Rian Hughes Device

"Art, Commercial"

*To my parents, Alan and Maureen,
who never once told me to get a proper job.*

A special thank you to all those sympathetic
clients that behave more like patrons; you
are the lifeblood of good design.

Device: Art, Commercial *by Rian Hughes*

Rian Hughes / Device:
www.devicefonts.co.uk
rianhughes.com
rianhughes@aol.com

Device fonts are available direct from the
Device website www.devicefonts.co.uk, or
via FontShop, FontWorks (UK) or [T-26].

Introduction | Grant Morrison
Foreword | Jim Davies
Afterword | Steve Cook
Editor | Robert Klanten

Rian Hughes photograph | John R. Ward
Rostrum photography | John R. Ward
Scanning | Orange
CD programming | Gary Newby

*Thank you to all those I have worked with
and for, and in particular:*
Paul Gravett, Tony and Carol Bennett, Nick
Landau, Leigh Baulch, Mike Lake, Pete
Hayward, Jo Mirosky, John Warwicker, Peter
Hogan, Mark Cox, Curtis King, Shelly Bond,
Maria Cabardo, Dean Motter, Julie
Rottenburg, Richard Bruning, Scott Dunbier,
Amie Brockway, Robbin Brosterman, Karen
Berger, Ian and Danny at Orange, Russel
Coultart, Glenn Mack, Kevin May, Hunt
Emerson, John Pasche, Dale Walker, Dave
Golden, Matt Bookman, Dick Hansom, Cefn
Ridout, Alan Moore, Frank Wynne, Grant
Morrison, Mark Millar, Jim Davies, John
Freeman, Chris Reynolds, Dave Gibbons,
Chris Foss, Lucio Santoro, David Leach, Nick
Lazarow, Markus Benton, John R. Ward, Andy
Dixon, Steven Cook, Alan McKenzie, Ever
Meulen, Steve MacManus, Mediumsize,
Edwina and Walkyman, Rudy Geeraerts,
Dale Crain, Rick Vermeulen, Banx, Daniel and
Didier Pasamonik, Eddie Campbell, Woodrow
(Trevs) Pheonix, Ed (Ilya) Hillyer, Ed Pinsent,
Javier Mariscal, Mike McMahon, FontShop,
FontWorks, Ken Cromb, Ellie and Saron,
Gilbert Shelton, Robert Crumb, Carlos
Segura, Mark Doyle, Rob O'Connor, Jaime
Hernandez, Jamie Hewlett, Fred Deakin,
Steven and Pablo, Bladdered by Fax, Huw
Thomas, Paul Adams, Lisa Nicholls, Malcolm
Garrett, Graham Storey, Leslie Weeks, Mark
Cornwell, Gary Newby, Shelly Warren,
Becky Glibbery and Ian Harrison.

The publishers and Rian Hughes would like
to thank the copyright holders for their
permission in allowing the use of their
material, and especially DC Comics,
Rebellion and Knockabout Comics.

Body text set in Paralucent, a Device font.

Some images are available for licencing.

Die Deutsche Bibliothek
CIP Einheitsaufnahme
Hughes, Rian:
Device: Art, Commercial
Rian Hughes – Berlin:
Die Gestalten Verlag, 2002
ISBN 3-931126-86-2

Printed by Medialis Offset, Berlin
Made in Europe

For your local dgv distributor please go to:
www.die-gestalten.de

Die Gestalten Verlag

Rian Hughes Device

Berlin

"Art, Commercial"

Foreword
Adventure Potholing

Today's youngsters probably won't remember the halcyon days of Wing Commander Rian 'Shaft' Hughes and Her Majesty's Royal Skywriter Squadron but ask your dad or grandad about the infamous, square-jawed 'Art Pilot of Tomorrow', and maybe the old man will have a few stories up his sleeve. For a while I thought we old duffers of the RSS had been completely forgotten in the race to replace the sky with the computer screen in the fight for the hearts and minds of the visually aware.

Back at the Fleet HQ, Hughes was always seen as a bit of a maverick but he became something of a schoolboy

hero for a while after transforming 1, 000 square miles of irrigated plain into a wry homage to Mondrian during the Chinese Cultural Revolution; Chairman Mao was particularly infuriated by Hughes' cheeky eau-de-Nil and peach combinations. These were 'anti-Socialist' colours which the Chinese leader hated to see together on the grounds that 'they violate my ethics, like the sound of old John Foxx records do.' Rian had the dashing good looks for all that press stuff and he was equally well known for his superhuman understanding of the colour theory which gave British Skywriters the edge over sensitive men like Mao.

This all goes back to a time when the Warsaw Pact and NATO were locked in a mad race to stay ahead of new developments in Global Graphic Design. We were all young lads ourselves then; daredevil types who fought and died to keep the home skies clear of enemy propaganda and other aerial graffiti attacks in the difficult-to-understand days between the deaths of Hitler and Diana.

Nowadays, when people can barely make sense of words at all and wouldn't know Surface-to-Art Combat if they saw it written down in front of them, it's very easy to be cynical about the value of sending young artists skyward to die incandescent deaths at the melting Ferrari-red controls of massive Color Saturation Bombers, blue-grey SuperStylus Fighters and all the other gleaming Frank Lloyd Wright-meets-Gerry Anderson myth-machines of the old Fleet. High-altitude verbal combat looks easy from the ground but try sketching an amusing 'Astronut'-style lampoon of the inevitable North Vietnamese surrender to capitalism while a Soviet NIB hunter/killer scrawls up hard on your tail, then talk to me and 'the Shaft' about the 'easy' life. Try a death tango in the upper levels of the stratosphere with smoky Cyrillic logos

wrapped around your fuselage and raw Letraset moire crackling away in the rearview and then maybe you'll earn my respect the way Rian Hughes earned my respect long ago.

We were the hand-picked elite of the nation's most progressive Airborne Art and Design schools, it's true. Even without Rian's incredible innovations and developments, Squadron technology was always at the very forefront of what would now be called 'state-of-the-art'. Back then, that meant hi-impact side-mounted diffuser nozzles, six Rolls Royce compressor engines with scalpel brackets, T-square

control bars and droop quill. Ejector seat. Font Bay dump doors with Serif tips for fine detail work. Nothing like the SuperStylus Fighter had ever been seen in the sky and its sleek line became the envy of every grey-flanneled young boy in the land. For a brief golden time all eyes were turned upward to read the messages and logos we printed in the air above their heads, thousands of feet beyond human reach.

And then the pre-digital world was over. The beautiful ink-spattered machines rusted in their hangars and the world moved on. Computers were easier to fly and had fewer wings to worry about. Anyone who still remembers 'Squiggles of the Squadron' from that wonderful old boy's weekly paper, 'The Ripper!' will no doubt have fond memories of the analogue adventures of those unforgettable superheroic skywriters.

But I was there.

Grant Morrison
Collaborator on *Dare, Doom Patrol, Really and Truly, Invisibles*

Introduction
The particle physics of design

The truly great names in graphic design tend to be individuals. Characterised by a personal vision and agenda, they are the sort who blur the disciplinary boundaries of the specialist and don't like to bow to the lazy dictates of commerce. During the 1970s and early 1980s this breed seemed threatened by extinction; corporate conformity did its best to stifle unorthodoxy, and mainstream design tended towards the blandly predictable.

This prevailing culture went against the grain for an up-and-coming generation weaned on the democratic principles of punk, which held that anyone could express themselves for three minutes, no matter how good, bad or different they happened to be. Among them was Rian Hughes; however, after graduating from the London College of Printing, his working life could hardly have started more inauspiciously. He arrived late at his very first job interview at a design and advertising agency with a lump of dog excrement stuck to the bottom of his portfolio, managed to transfer some of it on to the white shirt he was wearing and the rest onto the meeting-room table. Directors had to open windows to let the stench out. Despite this, he got the job. "However, I don't recommend this as an interview technique," he advises. Hughes went on to a succession of

short stints in advertising agencies, record sleeve design companies and publishing houses. He seemed to be looking for a good fit for his talents and interests, but while learning a lot along the way, not finding it. Highlights in this period included stints at *I-D* magazine (then art directed by Stephen Male), *Smash Hits*, Condé Nast (where he worked for a summer "on everything from *Tatler* to *House and Garden*"), and at music design studios Mainartery and da Gama, then fronted by Tomato's John Warwicker. During this period, a burgeoning freelance client list in illustration, design and comic strips was making a full-time job untenable.

It was while at Mainartery that the Belgian publisher Magic Strip offered Hughes his first book deal, a graphic novel titled *The Science Service* which he both co-wrote and drew. Published in seven languages, the book was to prove his decisive break into the comics industry, and led to work for Britain's *Revolver* magazine with 1990's *Dare*, a collaboration with writer Grant Morrison which iconoclastically revamped the 1950s comics hero Dan Dare ("a work of elegant beauty," said the *NME*). For *2000AD* Hughes then revived the old character *RoboHunter* with writer Peter Hogan, and co-created his own strips *Really & Truly* and *Tales From Beyond Science* (with writers Grant Morrison and Mark Millar). A demanding and complex medium, comics taught Hughes to develop and hone a number of skills: traditional life drawing ability, an eye for expressive body language, researching reference materials – and a knack for storytelling.

Hughes' experience of comic book art and graphic novels typifies his tendency to deconstruct the language of any given form he finds himself interested in, the better to understand it and then reconstruct it to his own specifications. "In comics, a well-developed language has been historically, through repeated use, mutually agreed: balloons show the

reader what people are saying but don't qualify as part of the picture, while the square dialogue box is read in a similar fashion to a voiceover in a film. Readers are fully conversant with these conventions, to the extent that they have become invisible." Hughes was fascinated by the expressive possibilities of tweaking these givens – in the *Really and Truly* strip, for example, he used a range of typefaces to signify the different voices of the protagonists.

At the same time, Hughes was engaged on design work for publishers Titan Books and Knockabout Comics, often repackaging classic comics material for the UK market. "I was attempting to inject a new design sensibility to a genre that had managed to ghettoise itself with outdated, inward-looking and formulaic packaging – and hopefully bring work like the Hernandez brothers' *Love and Rockets* and Robert Crumb to the wider and more sophisticated audience they deserved. It was something of a personal crusade." Many of Hughes' innovations were taken up by the original publishers for their own subsequent editions, and design work for American companies like DC Comics soon followed.

But for Hughes, actually drawing comics has been put on the back burner. "I got to the point where I was doing a great deal of non-strip work; advertising, illustration, type design, logo design - and I was offered *Adam Strange* at DC, which is something like 28 pages a month. You pretty much can't do anything else *but* that, and although it was something I really wanted to do, it meant that it would be the *only* thing I could do, so for the time being I had to turn my back on a regular comic book. I will definitely go back to it at some future date, but it's too constraining a thing to solely do and I wanted to explore all these other avenues as well."

Hughes' disregard of convention and definition extends across the full scope of his work. He deftly moves between design, typography, comics, illustration and even animation, considering them all parts of one interrelated continuum. There is plenty of historic precedent for this holistic approach to graphic design, notably the great poster artists of the 1930s, Cassandre and Jean Carlu, who combined type, image and layout to achieve a dynamic, integrated whole. "I would hope that if you are creative then you can be creative in lots of different areas," says Hughes. "They [clients] are not employing you solely for your technical skills, they're employing you for your quality of thinking... you don't want to be a stylist who people commission because they want a particular sheen laid across what they just happen to be doing." Hughes seems to have the attitude of an artist working in the commercial arena. "'Commercial Art' was the term for graphic design before graphic design was coined. 'Commercial Artists' were illustrators, typographers, designers... they were versatile. 'Art' and 'Commercial', wedded together, no questions asked. I like that."

Hughes is adamant that a mastery of drawing skills and technique should be an integral part of the designer's repertoire. As a child he was rarely seen without a pen or pencil in his hand, and this early natural proclivity was later combined with a mastery of the more

formal elements of composition, colour, shading and perspective. Over the years – on a host of posters, greetings cards, record sleeves and T-shirts – he has explored a wide range of different styles with a remarkable level of dexterity. Despite this breath of output, Hughes is probably best-known for his firm-jawed or tight-waisted figures, a contemporary take that has distant roots in the 'clear line' style of European illustrators like Ever Meulen and Serge Clerc. When he added digital techniques to the pen and brush the transition was made organically and smoothly, and resulted in a crisper, harder-edged aesthetic, a move away from outlines and an incorporation of more textural effects. Working in Adobe Illustrator and Photoshop, his use of strong flat planes of colour sometimes brings to mind a vogueish early 1960s look, though he insists "I don't like pastiche and I'm not trying to mimic any historical style." Regardless, Hughes' eye for telling detail and his wicked observational humour have remained constants.

When the Macintosh began to make its presence felt in design circles in the early 1980s, a common complaint was that designers were now expected to take on the additional burden of typesetting. To Hughes, this was a palpable bonus, allowing him to work

rigorously from the bottom up, and also adding welcome speed and immediacy. Hughes had already learnt the traditional mechanical artworking techniques: specifying type, marking up overlays and processing Chromalins, before having to come to grips with the early, and often temperamental, Macintosh. Tellingly, he belongs to the only generation to bridge the analogue/digital divide, appreciating the heritage, forethought and discipline of the former while enjoying the speed, liberation and flexibility of the latter.

Hughes has described typography as the "particle physics of design". Its ability to explore the relationship

between form and meaning at an elemental level, its nuances, its power to convey personality and emotion in a few eloquent strokes, makes it difficult for him to resist. His interest in letterforms began at an unusually young age, thanks to a Letraset catalogue his architect father had lying about the studio. It was then that he came to the realisation that there were designers who actually drew typefaces for a living, and he wrote to all the major photosetting companies of the time requesting catalogues.

That childhood fascination continued until, aged 15, he visited Letraset where for the first time he saw Rubylith being used to create type. "Each letter would be individually cut from this material, which is a thin red transparent masking film on a transparent base which you can cut with a weighted knife. You'd peel away the excess to reveal your letter, which was then photographed down and duplicated to make the Letraset master sheet. Alan Meeks at Letraset showed me how this was done and I was absolutely fascinated. The fine degree of control, the technical facility these guys had... they were experts at cutting the most intricate shapes out of this stuff." This was the technique Hughes used in the early days of his career to produce custom type for his design work: "Pre

Mac, I'd cut letters out of Rubylith at a large size and PMT them down, then cut them out and reassemble them into the headlines I needed by pasting them onto board. This would then be copied a second time. It was all a very longwinded, laborious and rather tedious process. The early fonts like Crash Bang Wallop and Revolver (originally designed for *Speakeasy* and *Revolver* magazines respectively) were digitisations of fonts I had originally done in this old-fashioned cut-and-paste method."

Hughes is prolific to say the least. Still in his 30s, he has created literally hundreds of fonts in a broad range of styles. He insists that all of them adhere to a set of strict self-imposed guidelines: that each font, however different – within their own context – is self-consistent and resolved. His first fonts were released in 1992 as part of the FontFont range, but then he decided to go it alone with his own foundry, Device Fonts. "I had a large backlog of fonts derived from my own work that I had been using on magazines such as *Deadline* for some time. They didn't exist as whole international character sets at that point; they just had what I needed. I spent some time completing the full character complement, then launched the first one hundred all under the Device foundry banner in 1995."

Many of Hughes' fonts were created for specific design commissions, and their names reflect their application or the circumstances of their conception. The chunky no-nonsense, hard-as-nails Judgement family was commissioned for *2000AD*, home of Judge Dredd. The jaunty Metropol Noir, which was created specifically for the 1996 MTV Europe Music Awards programme, is named after the Paris hotel Hughes was put up in for the event. Others are more descriptive: Knobcheese suggests Swiss cheese, and Foonky and Laydeez Night derive from the kitsch 1970s aesthetic Hughes was brought up on and to which he remains so attached. He has admitted that some, perhaps for sentimental reasons, are named after old girlfriends, but maintains that font names – whether frivolous or 'serious' – should indicate intention of use by being descriptive. Blackcurrant for example, derived from lettering executed for the Japanese fashion chain Yellow Boots, is the kind of typeface you might expect to find on fruit pastille packaging.

Again, there is a kind of cultural ping-pong at work here. Hughes admits to being attracted by the pop iconography of certain types of packaging: bubble gum wrappers, soft drinks, washing powder boxes, and so on. He'll perhaps create a typeface inspired by such an

aesthetic – after analysing it, deconstructing it, putting his own slant on it – and eventually, completing the circle, it may actually end up being used on another, similar, piece of packaging.

His relationship with, and attitude towards, advertising is even more involved. On the one hand, he is happy to contribute to a mass medium where his work is widely showcased and successfully fulfils a given function; on the other he remains mystified by the mindset that drives some full-time advertising practitioners ("when they were kids, was it really their ambition to sell more, say, peanuts when they grew up?"). However, Hughes recognises that there are valuable lessons to be learnt from the direct approach that advertising demands. "It teaches you clarity, succinctness, the need to make yourself understood quickly and effectively. Meaningless mark-making, gratuitous decoration and a failure to fully grasp the way people read and understand your work are anathema."

Ultimately, and in all the various manifestations of his work, Hughes' aim is to communicate with his audience on an elemental level. In this sense, he is a modernist: he feels there may be an almost Platonic, universal aesthetic order. While clothed in the subject matter of culture, the underlying abstracted forms – shapes and colours, textures and composition – combine to achieve an instinctively understood emotional resonance. His work, he says, is an ongoing investigation to understand and unlock this fundamental visual language, to discover how it works, and why. "Are we uncovering nature or inventing it? Is the 'rightness' that you arrive at in a work an invention or discovery? Is its appeal a reflection of the way our brains are wired – to seek sense – or a deeper insight into the structure of nature?"

"On the surface it seems to be very simple, but it's actually mysterious and complex," he says. "It all comes down to what we consider to be beauty; these abstract notions of harmony, the 'tautness' that comes between imbalance and balance, between the verbal / symbolic and the aesthetic – what things look like and what they mean. It is these visual relationships that design, illustration and especially typography are so good at embodying. A good analogy for design is music. There's the intellectual, rational side to it and there's the emotional, intuitive side. What I'm trying to produce is the visual equivalent of that chord change that makes the hairs on the back of your neck stand up."

Jim Davies

| Item descriptions conform to the conventions of comics: left to right, top to bottom.
| All design, art direction, illustration, photography and typography are by Rian Hughes unless additional credits show otherwise.

Rian Hughes (as much as I hate to admit it in print) is a vector virtuoso.

With all the fonts I commissioned for 2000AD over the years he would hand me at least ten ideas and a whole stack of extra dingbats. It has to be said, though, I never did find a use for the condom or steaming turd icons.

Rian delivers. The only time he didn't rise to the occasion was his tragic attempt at paragliding. After assuring me endlessly that he'd have no problem landing on the beach, I watched him plummet into 20ft of Pacific Ocean... but not before he was seen frantically trying to roll up his trouser legs.

Such is his determination.

You can always have a good time working with Rian but never, ever, under any circumstances do you mess with this man's kerning.

Steve (Robo)Cook
*Art director and designer, 2000AD
progs 555-1273*

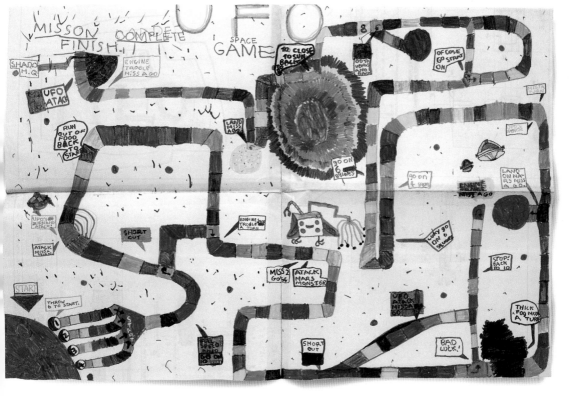

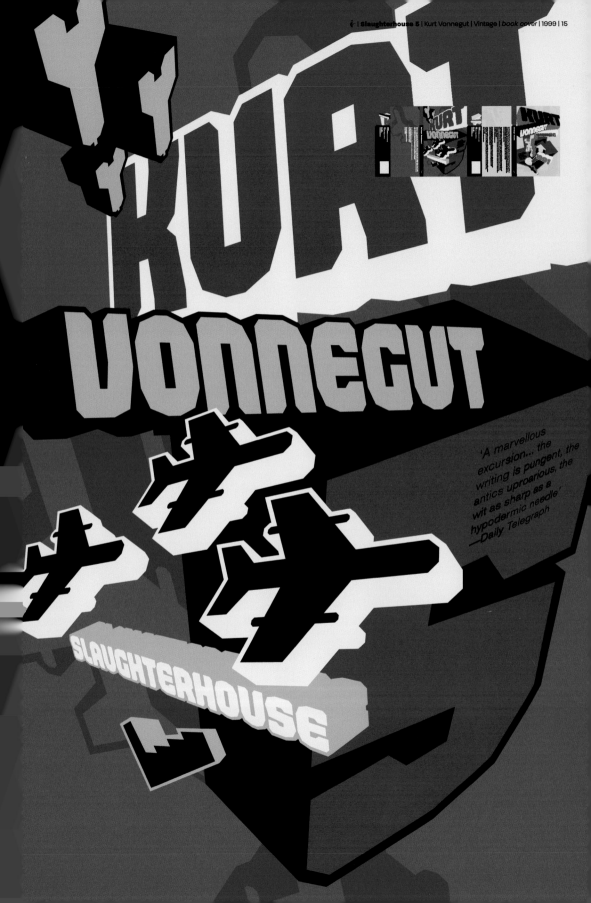

KURT VONNEGUT

SLAUGHTERHOUSE

'A marvellous excursion... the writing is pungent, the antics uproarious, the wit as sharp as a hypodermic needle'
—Daily Telegraph

Royal Festival Hall
Queen Elizabeth Hall
Purcell Room

5-25 April 2001
La Linea
London's
Latin Music
Festival

Including
Omara Portuondo
Cubanismo
Ozomatli
Orishas
Cachaito

020 960 4242
WWW.RFH.ORG.UK

Royal Festival Hall
Queen Elizabeth Hall
Purcell Room

5-25 April 2002
La Linea
London's
Latin
Music
Festival

Including
Omara Portuondo
Cubanismo
Ozomatli
Orishas
Cachaito

rianhughes@aol.com
www.deviesfonts.co.uk

020 960 4242
WWW.RFH.ORG.UK

www.freakboarders.com

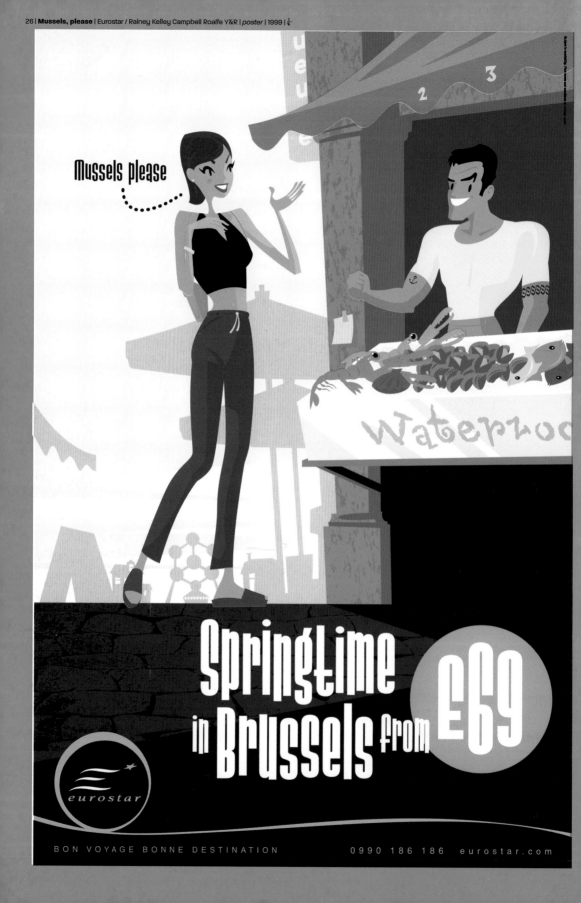

| Louvre / Horseracing / Frog's Legs | Eurostar / Rainey Kelley Campbell Roalfe Y&R | *press advertisements* | 1999 |

𝕚 | **Planetsavers** | Friends of the Earth | informational booklet | *cover* | 1998 | 31
Virus protection | Mac User | *editorial illustration* | 1995 |
Tyro Typo | FontShop | FontBook divider | *illustration* | 1993 |

AUTOMATIC ANTHEMS
NEW BRITISH HOUSE

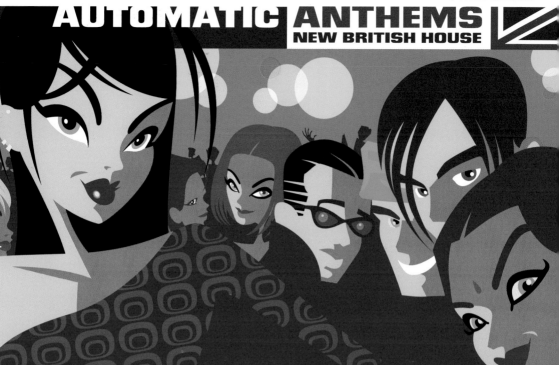

1 ready to receive 2 small space 3 ?? 4 animal house 5 wasted 6 animal
7 speakeasy 8 silence 9 sodium glow 10 sunday driver 11 always be 12 don't look away

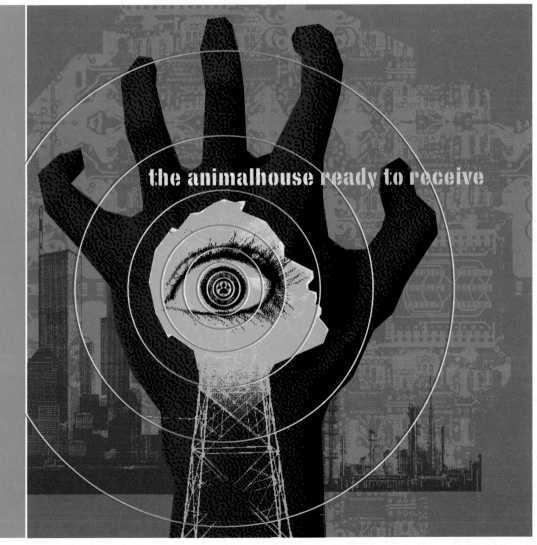

SC090
Design: Rian Hughes ©1999
Printed on paper from managed Scandinavian forests

christmas
joy

christmas
cheer

two thousand
greetings

christmas
bliss

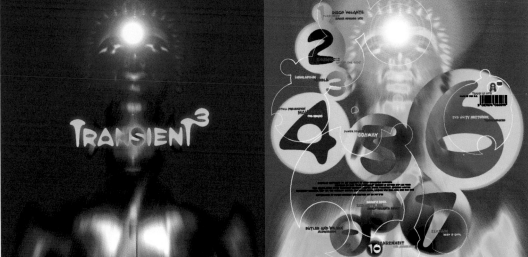

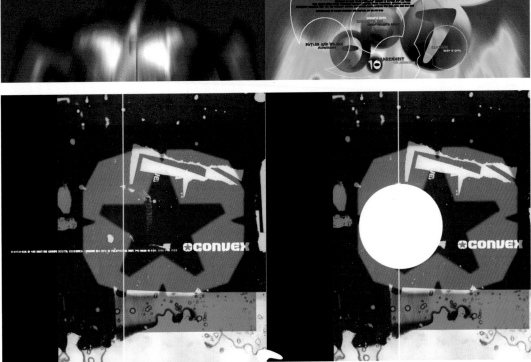

52 | **John "00" Fleming** | Licenced to Thrill | Automatic | CD album | 1998 |
| design and art direction: Rian Hughes | photography: John R. Ward |
| inset: photo session unretouched polaroid

MI CHICO LATINO GERI HALLIWELL
WRITTEN BY HALLIWELL/WATKINS/WILSON. PUBLISHED > WINDSWEPT PACIFIC MUSIC LTD/19 MUSIC/BMG. PRODUCED > ABSOLUTE. ENGINEERED >
PAUL 'P-DUB' WALTON. ADDITIONAL PROGRAMMING > MIKE HIGHAM. MIXED > MARK 'SPIKE' STENT. ASSISTED > WAYNE WATKINS.
℗1999 THE COPYRIGHT IN THIS SOUND RECORDING IS OWNED BY EMI RECORDS LTD. ©1999 EMI RECORDS THIS LABEL COPY INFORMATION
IS THE SUBJECT OF COPYRIGHT PROTECTION. ALL RIGHTS RESERVED. ©1999 EMI RECORDS. FOR PROMOTIONAL USE ONLY NOT FOR RESALE. CDEMDJ 508

FRANKIE'S ROMEO

RUTH LOUISE SYMES

FRANKIE'S BOYFRIEND IS A ROBOT.

FRANKIE SWORE SHE HAD A BOY-FRIEND WHEN SHE DIDN'T. OOPS!

SO WHEN SHE FOUND A BODY IN A BOX IN HER GRAN'S LABORATORY, SHE PUT THE BITS TOGETHER TO MAKE ONE.

BUT BEING THE GIRLFRIEND OF A GORGEOUS HUNK ISN'T EASY - ESPECIALLY WHEN THE HUNK IS ROMEO, A ROBOT WITH ATTITUDE.

A LAUGH-A-MINUTE STORY ABOUT HOW ONE LITTLE LIE CAN LAND A GIRL IN A WHOLE HEAP OF TROUBLE.

A Dolphin ★ Paperback

£4.99 UK
$8.99 CANADA

FRANKIE'S ROMEO

RUTH LOUISE SYMES

62 | **Visitors from Oz** | Martin Gardner | Penguin | *book cover* | 1998 | ✦
| **The Secret Paris of the 1930s** | Brassaï | Unpublished college project | *book cover* | 1984
| **Lola Comes Home** | Claudine Cullimore | Penguin | *book cover* | 2000

E. M. FORSTER

A Room with a View

E.M. FORSTER

A Room with a View

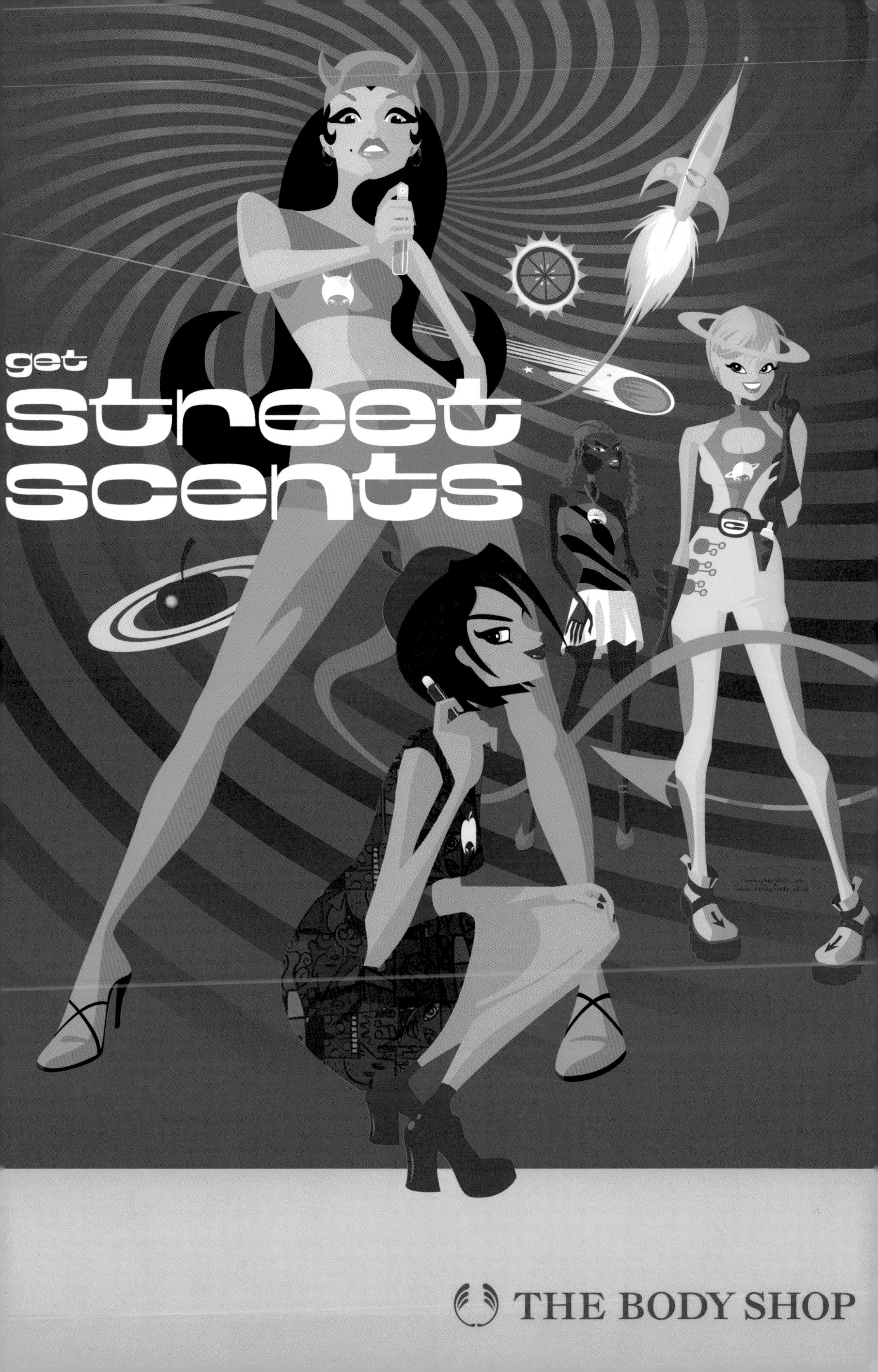
get
street
scents
THE BODY SHOP

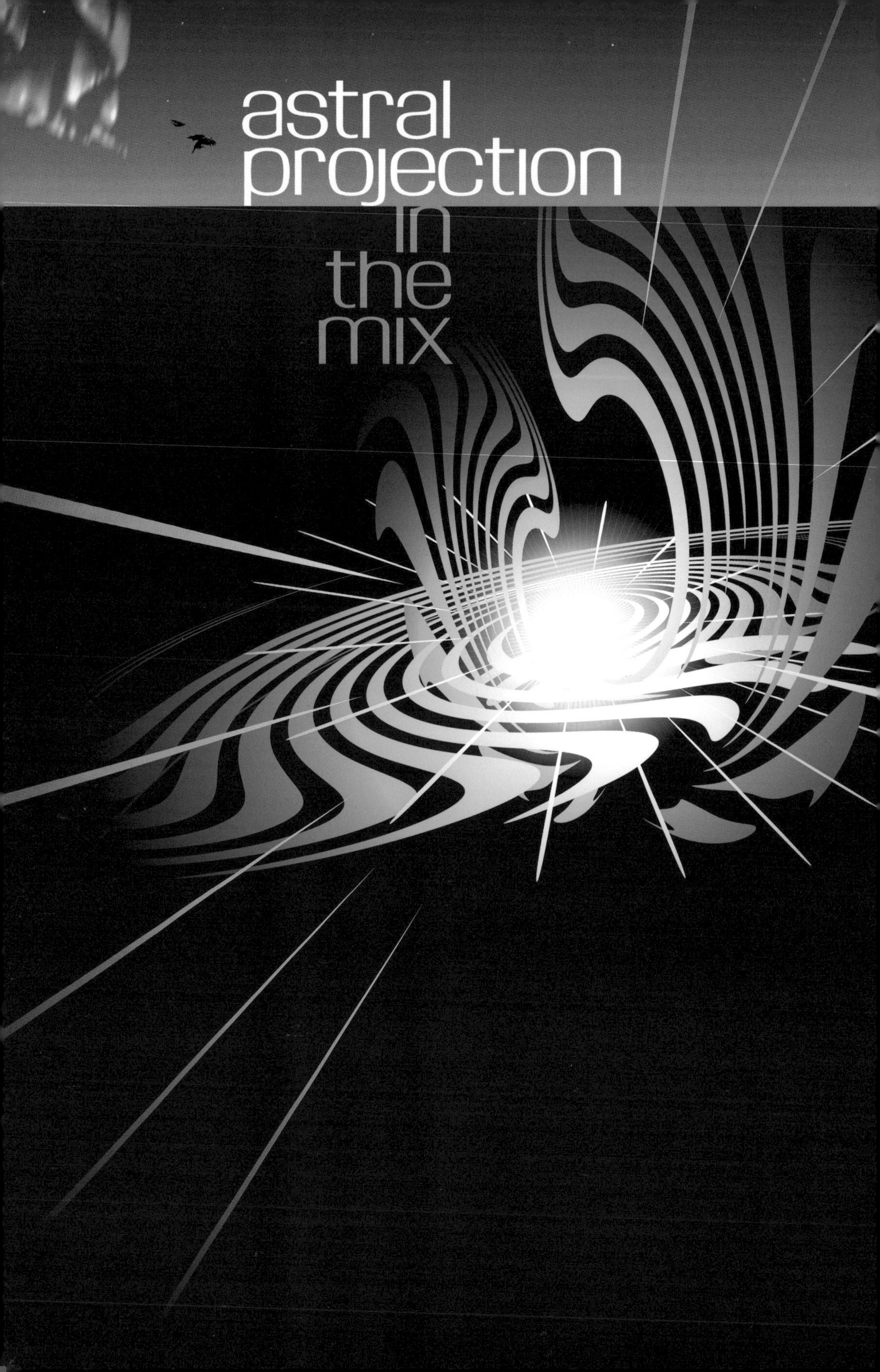
astral
projection
in
the
mix

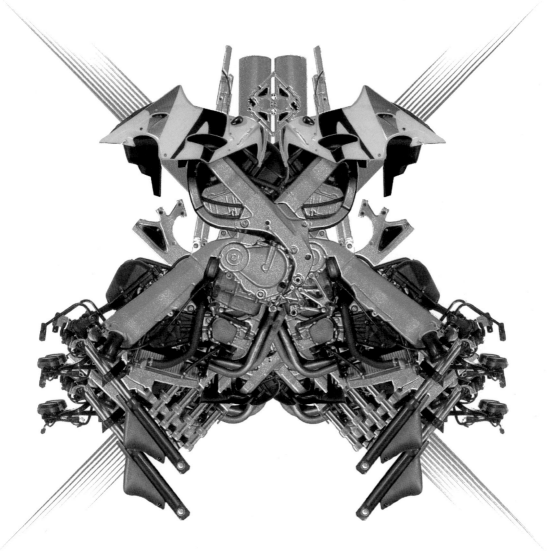

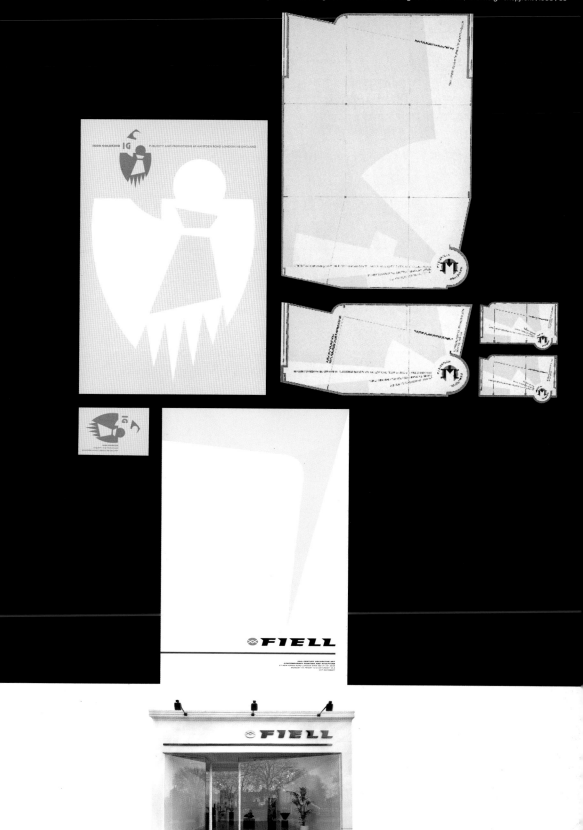

AUTO 8 CD

DREAMING OF YOU (RADIO EDIT) DREAMING OF YOU (QUIETMAN REMIX)
DREAMING OF YOU (MANTRA MIX) DREAMING OF YOU (ORIGINAL MIX)

Control Z: Dreaming of You

Automatic records

WRITTEN AND PRODUCED BY LESZEK GASIOREK
℗ 1998 AUTOMATIC RECORDS
© 1998 AUTOMATIC RECORDS
PUBLISHING: COPYRIGHT CONTROL

MADE IN THE U. K.

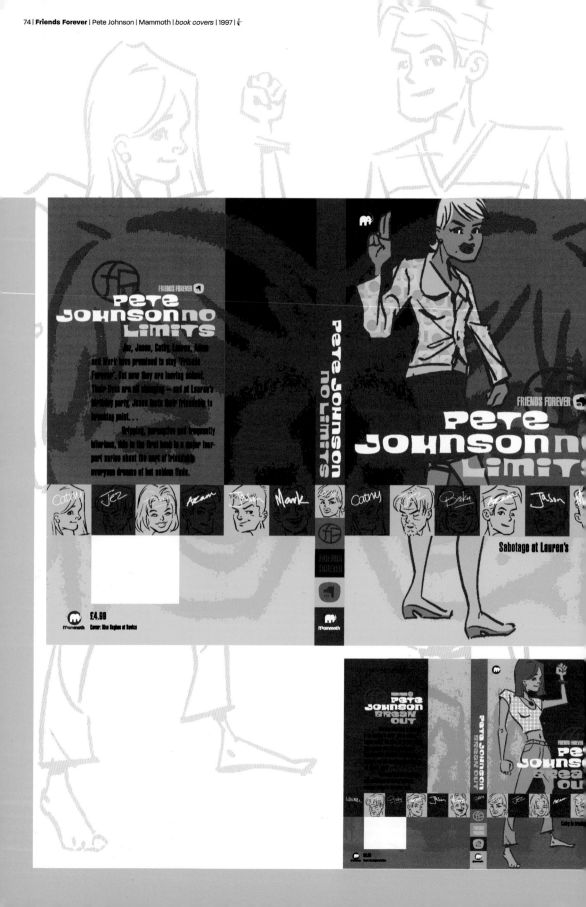

| **The Lie Spider** | Pippa Goodheart | Mammoth | *book cover* | 1997 | 75
Gloria's Gramophone | Akulah Akbami | Mammoth | *book cover* | 1996 |
Friends Forever | Pete Johnson | Mammoth | *book covers* | 1997 |

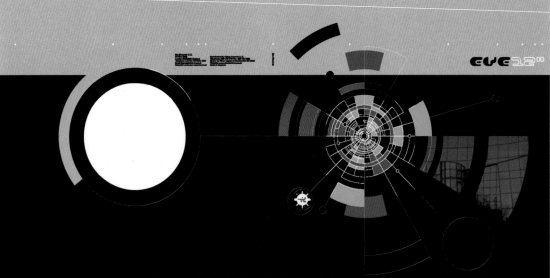

Soulflash Dubs | Shark Infested Waters | Soulflash | *12" single* | 1997 |
Three Colours | Sitting Pretty | Soul Selects | *12" single* | 1987 |
design and art direction: Rian Hughes | illustration: Rian Hughes |
Three Colours | This is Norwood | Soul Selects | *album* | 1987 |
design: Rian Hughes | photograph: unknown |

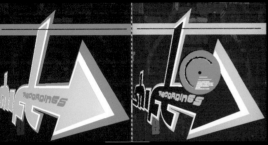

A1018

For the different sides of you

CRIME ALWAYS PAYS

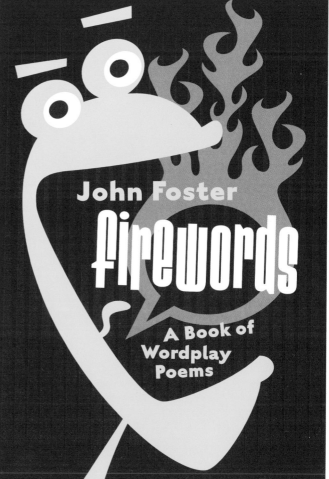

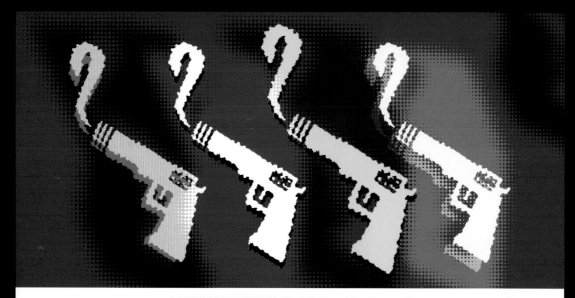

ADVERTISING SMOKING KILLS
TOBACCO IS ADVERTISING'S BIGGEST BILLBOARD CLIENT
TOBACCO KILLS MORE THAN FOUR TIMES AS MANY PEOPLE AS AIDS, FIREARMS AND DRUG ABUSE COMBINED
Chief Medical Officer's Warning

Save
on
Hotpoint
in our
Winter
Sale

and you can
afford
to be
reckless

102 | **Senza Faccia** | Eve | *LP proposal* | 1997 |
| design and art direction: Rian Hughes | blue faces painting: Sante Arrē
| **Girotondo** | Eve | *CD album* | 1998
| design and art direction: Rian Hughes | original spiral drawing: Sante Arrē
| **Girotondo** | Eve | *LP* | 1998
| design and art direction: Rian Hughes | original spiral drawing: Sante Arrē

Warner Bros. Reprise Guide | Warner Bros. / Mike Diehl | *CD sampler* | 2001 | 103
Stock Aitken Waterman | Roadblock | A&M | *12" single* | 1987 |
Smith and Mighty | Remember Me | London Records | *12" single proposal* | 1994 |
Kirsty MacColl | Mambo de la Luna | V2 / Stylorouge | *7" single proposal* | 1999 |
Clever Kids | Atmosphere | *CD sampler* | 1995 |
Fun, Fun, Fun | Atmosphere | *CD sampler* | 1997 |
Mad, Bad and Jazzy 2 | Atmosphere | *CD sampler* | 1999 |

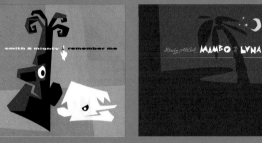

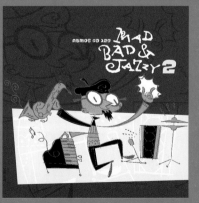

104 | **Deadline** | *magazine design* | 1995 |
| design and art direction: Rian Hughes | cover illustrations: Issue 69 Jamie Hewlett | 70 Steve Whitaker | 71 Ilya
| **Deadline** | Dead Lucky | *section header icon* |

| Deadline | *magazine design* | 1995 | 105
design and art direction: Rian Hughes | Chimera photograph: Phil Nicholls | other photographs supplied uncredited |
Deadline | Arrow icons | *magazine turns and ends* | 1995 |

106 | **Deadline** | *magazine design* | 1995 | &
| design and art direction: Rian Hughes | photographs supplied uncredited
| **Deadline** | Article endstop / Dead On / T-shirts / Dead Acres (letters) / Zines / Plug City | *section header icons* | 1995

Imacsploitation! | Mac User magazine | *cover* | 1999 | 108

House Party | New Woman magazine | *covermounted compilation CD* | 2000 | 109

Abstract 16 | FontShop / Device images | *royalty-free CD image (background image)* | 2001 |

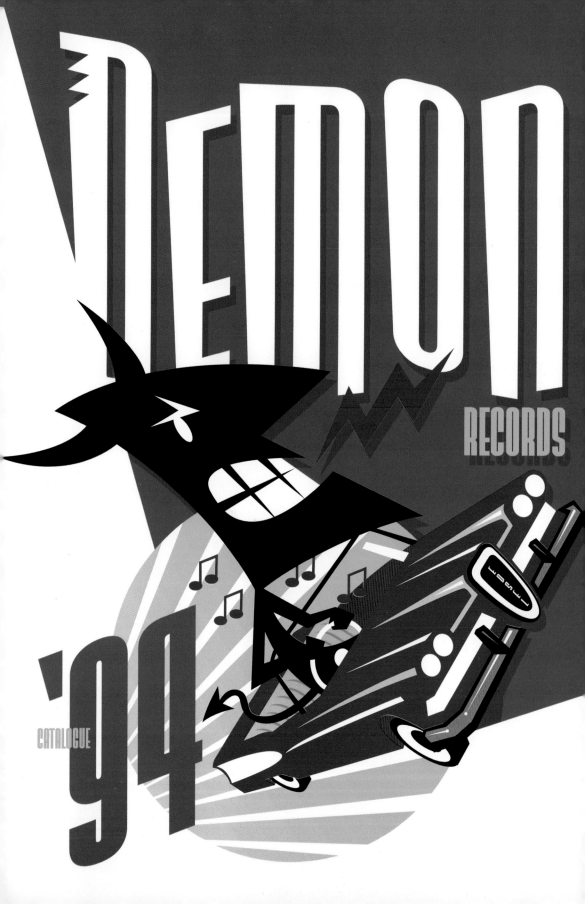

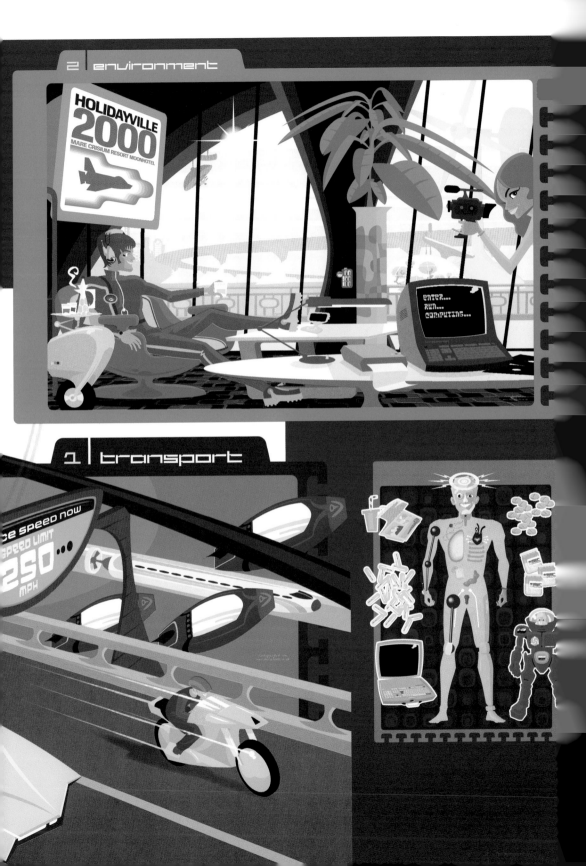

FOND: WhyTwoKay. Style: Plain. ID: 2000. Type: PS

MillenniumGreetings

Sample line settings

6 pt.	
7 pt.	
8 pt.	
9 pt.	
10 pt.	
12 pt.	
14 pt.	

48 pt.

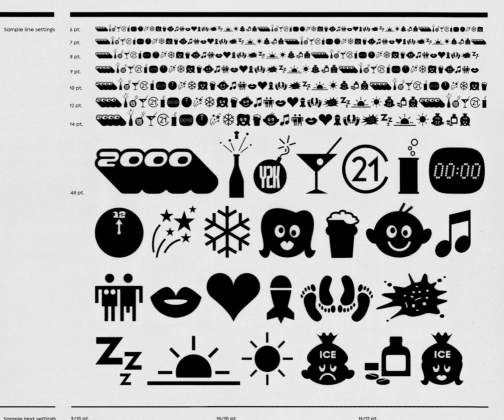

Sample text settings

9/10 pt.

10/10 pt.

11/12 pt.

Point size:	6	7	8	9	10	11	12	13	18	20	24	36	40
Chars/Pica:	4.82	4.14	3.61	3.21	2.9	2.63	2.41	2.23	1.61	1.44	1.2	0.8	0.5
Cap Height:	5mm	10mm	15mm	20mm	25mm	30mm	35mm	40mm	45mm	50mm	55mm	60mm	65mm
Approx. pt. size:	19.44	38.9	58.35	77.79	97.25	116.69	136.14	155.59	175.04	194.48	213.94	233.38	271.21

Maxim journalist

Film director

Racing driver

Professional gambler

Prince of Darkness

Bounty hunter

Private detective

Spin doctor

Navy Seal

Band manager

FBI agent

Cybermillionaire

Paranormal investigator

Slumming Royal

Payback

FF Crash Bang Wallop Light, Light Italic, **Medium, Medium Italic, Contoured**, Highlight. Orignal medium weight designed for A+M Records, 1987. Used subsequently for cover lines on Speakeasy magazine 1990. Released by Fontshop, 1993. © Rian Hughes / Fontshop 1993. Poster designed by Rian Hughes / device

**FF RIAN'S DINGBATS
ONE, TWO, THREE AND FOUR**
DESIGNED BY
RIAN HUGHES ©1993
AVAILABLE FROM
FONTSHOP INTERNATIONAL

by Rian Hughes. Part of the **Device** collection.

This text set in *Regulator*. Two sets of five and six fonts for $162 and $180.
© Rian Hughes. E-mail: rianhughesATaol.com

A typeface in the Swiss
(cheese) tradition.
With knobs on.

☞ FF Knobcheese ☜
☞ FF Knobcheese Outline ☜
☞ FF KNOBCHEESE INITIALS ☜

Designed by Rian Hughes ©1992. Available from Fontshop 1994. Best used with a cheap Burgundy.

0123456789ABCDEFGHIJKLMNOPQRSTUVWXYZabcdefghijklmnopqrstuvwxyz
ÀÁÂÃÄÅÇÈÉÊËÌÍÎÏÑÒÓÔÕÖØÙÚÛÜÝàáâãäåçèéêëìíîïñòóôõöøùúûüÿ
!?"#@$¢£ƒ%&'()°•,-./:;®•ffi★†☞‰<=>[\]-_`{|}-|°|@™®©2¥♠→÷+†©♦♣;♥♠♦☀«»,--""''‡§‡/¤†‰,   ª

| **Knobcheese** | FontShop | *poster* | 1992 | 128

Menswear | Device | *postcard* | 1998 | 129
Revolver | FontShop | *poster* | 1992 |
Identification | FontShop | *poster* | 1992 |

132 | **Space Lounge 2** | La Rocka / BC Ethic | *Hawaiian shirt proposal* | 2000 |
| **Riviera Fling 2** | La Rocka / BC Ethic | *Hawaiian shirt proposal* | 2000
| **Blaxploitation** | La Rocka / BC Ethic | *Hawaiian shirt* | 2000
| **Kung-fu Gorillas vs. Ufonauts** | La Rocka / BC Ethic | *Hawaiian shirt* | 2000
| **Blaxploitation** | *sleeve and back pattern (background image)* | 2000

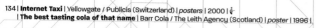

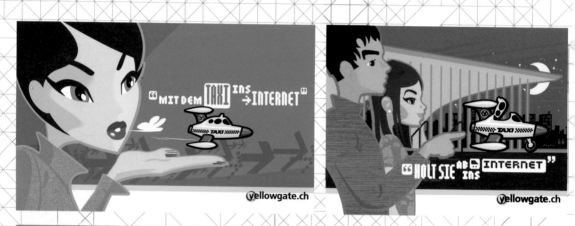

134 | **Internet Taxi** | Yellowgate / Publicis (Switzerland) | *posters* | 2000 |
| **The best tasting cola of that name** | Barr Cola / The Leith Agency (Scotland) | *poster* | 1996 |

135 | **She's gorgeous... but she stinks!** | Sure / Ammirati Puris Lintas | *poster* | 1999

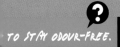

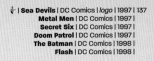 | **Sea Devils** | DC Comics | *logo* | 1997 | 137
Metal Men | DC Comics | 1997 |
Secret Six | DC Comics | 1997 |
Doom Patrol | DC Comics | 1997 |
The Batman | DC Comics | 1998 |
Flash | DC Comics | 1998 |

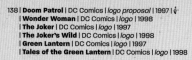

| The Batman | DC Comics | *logo proposal* | 1997 | 143
Tangent corporate and legal information logos | DC Comics | *logos* | 1997 |
Lex Luthor | DC Comics | *logo* | 1998 |
Mystery in Space | DC Comics | *logo proposals* | 1998 |
Mystery in Space | DC Comics | *logo* | 1998 |
The Unseen Hand | DC Comics | *logo* | 1996 |
The Unseen Hand | DC Comics | *logo proposal* | 1996 |

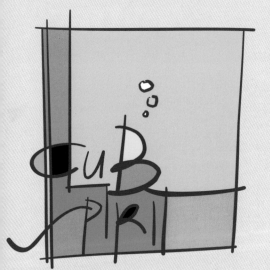

146 | **Blag** | Ministry of Sound | *theme night logo proposals* | 2000 | ♟
| **Hepcat Events** | Event promotion company | *logo* | 2001
| **Convex Records** | *logo proposals* | 1997
| **Scene of the Crime** | DC Comics | *logo* | 1999
| **Human Target** | DC Comics | *logo proposal* | 1998

148 | Predigital logo design selection | ✏

| **Canardo** | Fleetway / Xpresso Books | comic album | *logo* | 1991
| **Fax User** | Aaron Witkin | *magazine masthead* | 1987
| **Mylar Snug** | Speakeasy | *magazine mascot* | 1989
| **Doc Chaos** | Vortex Comics | *logo* | 1987
| **Jazz Funnies** | Knockabout Comics | comic album | *logo* | 1985
| **Crack** | Crack Editions / Knockabout Comics | comic imprint | *logo* | 1996
| **Titan Books** | Titan Books | science fiction and comic imprint | *logo* | 1985
| **Manowar** | Sign of the Hammer | 10 Records | *LP logo* | 1984
| **Midnight's Children** | 2000AD | comic series | *logo* | 1990
| **Starship Enterprises** | Starship Enterprises | Tour program publishers | *logo* | 1987
| **Doc Chaos** | Vortex Comics | *logo* | 1987
| **The Towers of Bois-Maury** | Titan Books | comic album | *logo* | 1989
| **Hellblazer** | Titan Books | comic album | *logo proposal* | 1989
| **Lord Jim** | Crisis magazine / Fleetway | comic series | *logo* | 1992
| **Batman Classics** | Titan Books | comic album | *logo proposal* | 1987
| **Xpresso Books man** | Fleetway | comic album imprint and magazine | *logo* | 1990
| **Speakeasy** | John Brown Publishing | *magazine masthead* | 1987
| **Mr. Positive** | Computer manufacturer | advertising campaign | *logo* | 1992
| **AARGH!** | Artists against rampant government homophobia | *logo* | 1988
| **Double Zero** | Double Zero | independent club night | *logo* | 1987
| **Peter Pank** | Knockabout Comics | comic album | *logo* | 1986
| **Xpresso Heads** | Fleetway | comic album imprint and magazine | *icons* | 1991
| **Xpresso** | Fleetway | *magazine masthead* | 1990
| **Firkin** | Knockabout Comics | comic album | *logo proposal* | 1995
| **Chopper** | Fleetway | comic album | *logo* | 1990
| **Video Browser** | Video viewing post | *logo* | 1992
| **Junker** | 2000AD comic | *series logo* | 1992
| **Xpresso Books** | Fleetway | comic album imprint | *logo* | 1990
| **AIV** | AIV | Skateboard team | *logo* | 1987
| **Judge Death** | The Judge Dredd Megazine | Fleetway | *series logo* | 1993
| **Rapid Reflexes** | Knockabout Comics | comic album | *logo* | 1991
| **Hellblazer** | Titan Books | comic album | *logo* | 1989

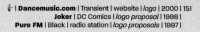
| **Dancemusic.com** | Transient | website | *logo* | 2000 | 151
Joker | DC Comics | *logo proposal* | 1998 |
Pure FM | Black | radio station | *logo proposals* | 1997 |

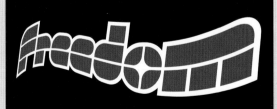

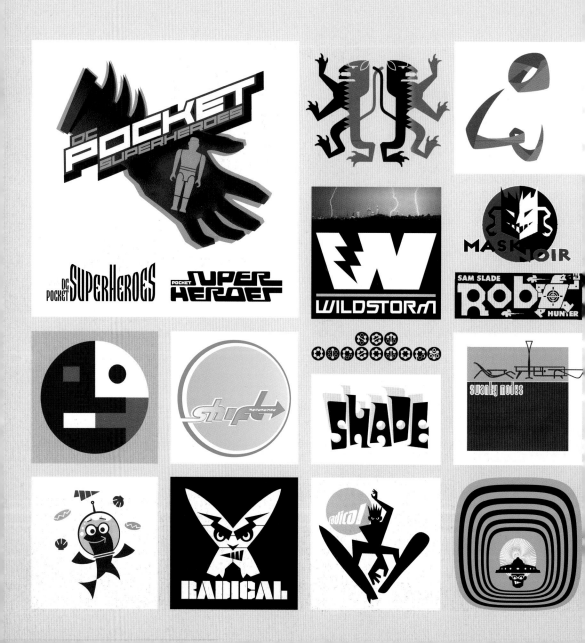

| Top 10 / Industry Quotes / Answers / Laptops / Mutimedia / By the Numbers / **Cutting Edge** | PC World magazine | *section headers* | 1996 | 161 |

XS | Extreme sport travel company | *logo proposals* | 1997 |

Can you hear me? | Orange | contract magazine | *diagrams* | 1997 |

Soda Club | Stylorouge / Concept Music | *logo proposal* | 2001 |

Device rubdown | Device fonts | Font digital retail website title | *logo* | 1998 |

My Little Pony | Hasbro UK | logo and brand development | *proposals* | 1999 |

174 | **Metropolitan Music** | *12" house bag* | 1995 | ♪
| **Metropolitan Music** | *12" onbody labels* | 1995-99 |
| design and art direction: Rian Hughes | photography: Rian Hughes

07/09/01
MIXED ABILITY

☐☐☐☐☐ Mirjam Buergin   Private View
☐☐☐☐☐ Alicia Duffy.   Friday 7 September 2001
☐☐☐☐☐ Andrew Grassie   6-9pm
☐☐☐☐☐ Peter Harris
☐☐☐☐☐ Saron Hughes   Late bar featuring
☐☐☐☐☐ Jasper Joffe   The Bowling Green DJ
☐☐☐☐☐ Rosanna Negrotti   and live music from
☐☐☐☐☐ Catharine O'Shea   The Caesar Romero Affair
☐☐☐☐☐ George Shaw
☐☐☐☐☐ Matthew Smith   Exhibition runs 8-14 September
☐☐☐☐☐ Charlotte Wales   Open daily 11am-6pm
ABCPF   Corsica Studios
                          28 Midland Road, NW1
                          5 minutes King's Cross tube

                          Press: 07944 976827
                          Telephone: 020 7380 1020
                          abilitymixed@hotmail.com
                          www.corsicastudios.com

YORK WAY
KING'S CROSS
PANCRAS ROAD
MIDLAND ROAD

CORSICA STUDIOS

𓅓 | **Travel games** | Chad Valley / Identica | *toy packaging* | 1995 | 177
Spiral Sketch | Chad Valley / Identica | *toy packaging* | 1995 |
Danny Rampling | Love Groove Dance Party | Metropole Music | *CD packaging* | 1996 |
art direction: Jenny Rampling | design: Rian Hughes | photography: Jenny Rampling / various |
Corn Flakes / Puffed Wheat | Marks and Spencer | *cereal packaging proposal* | 1998 |

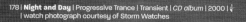

NIGHT AND DAY
PROGRESSIVE TRANCE
compiled by Mark Allen and Greg Lunar

| Cosmosis | Moonshine | Transient | *CD single* | 1996 | 179
Transient | *12" house bag proposal* | 2000 |
Transient | *12" house bag proposal* | 2001 |
Transient 8 | *CD album proposal* | 2001 |
Transient | *12" house bag* | 1997 |

TRANSIENT

180 | **Lucy Skye** | Feel of Fire (denim edition) | Mercury Records | *12" single sleeve* | 2000 | 🔦
 | **Lucy Skye** | Feel of Fire (suede edition) | Mercury Records | *12" single sleeve* | 2000
 | **Lucy Skye** | Feel of Fire | Mercury Records | *CD single* | 2000

| **Batman: Y. Joker** | Bob Hall with Lee Loughridge | DC Comics | book cover | 199
design and art direction: Rian Hughes | original illustration: Bob Hal

The Invisibles: say you want a revolution | Grant Morrison and various | DC Comics | *book cover* | 1996
design and art direction: Rian Hughes | figures adapted from an original illustration by Steve Yeowel

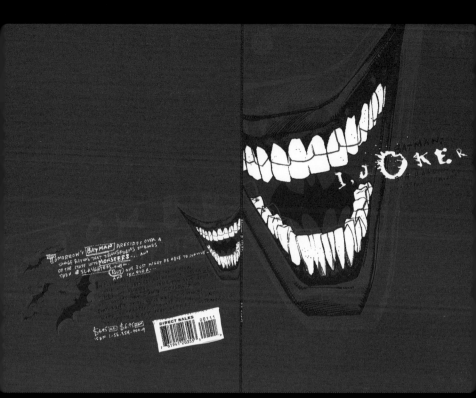

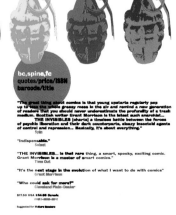

bc,spine,fc
quotes/price/ISSN
barcode/title

"The great thing about comics is that young upstarts regularly pop
up to toss the whole greasy mess in the air and remind a new generation
of readers that you should never underestimate the profundity of a trash
medium. Scottish writer Grant Morrison is the latest such anarchist...
THE INVISIBLES [charts] a timeless battle between the forces
of psychic liberation and their dark counterparts, sleazy insectoid agents
of control and repression... Basically, it's about everything."
Spin

"Indispensable."
Select

"THE INVISIBLES... is that rare thing, a smart, spooky, exciting comic.
Grant Morrison is a master of smart comics."
Time Out

"It's the next stage in the evolution of what I want to do with comics"
Grant Morrison

"Who could ask for more?"
Cleveland Plain-Dealer

$17.50 USA $34.00 Canada
ISBN 1-56389-267-2

Suggested for Mature Readers

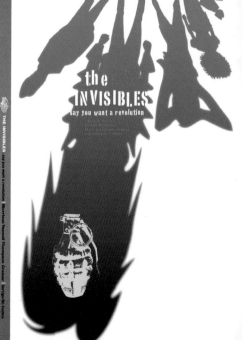

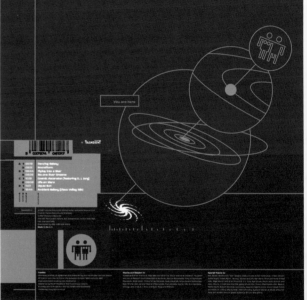

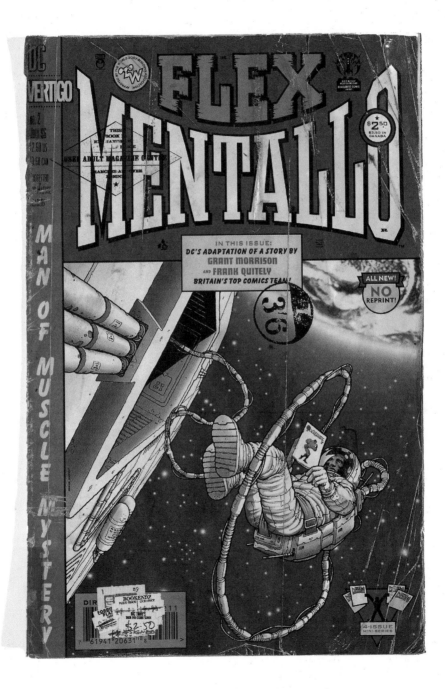

👤 | **Outbreaks of Violets** | MTV Europe Music Awards 1996 | *brochure, standard edition* | 1996 | 187
Outbreaks of Violets | MTV Europe Music Awards 1996 | *brochure, limited edition* | 1996 |
design and art direction: Rian Hughes | text: Alan Moore | production editor: Frank Wynne |
illustrations: Max Cabanes / Ever Meulen / John Burns / Jamie Hewlett / Max / Rachel Ball / Ed Pinsent /
Javier Mariscal / Avril / Mike McMahon / Mique Beltran / Jean Phillipe Stassen / Kellie Strom / Isabel Krietz /
Max Andersson / Stefano Ricci / Francois Bouq / Edouard Boudoin / Pirinen / Lorenzo Mattoti / Christian Gorney |

Billy Tipton's Secret

People who know jazz music know the name of Billy Tipton. The baby-faced Tipton played both saxophone and piano for legendary big bands headed by Jack Teagarden and Ross Carlyle in the '30s and '40s.

The Billy Tipton Trio formed in 1954 with Dick O'Neal on drums and Ron Kilde on bass. They were a successful group for over ten years.

In 1960, Tipton met Kitty Oakes, a shapely red-headed exotic dancer.

Wow! What a dish!

Soon afterwards, Tipton was telling all his friends that Kitty was now Mrs. Tipton.

Within a few years the Tiptons adopted three boys.

Tipton was a good father. He took the kids camping and even became a scoutmaster.

Being a good scout will help you learn to be a man.

In the late '90s, Tipton fell ill but refused to seek medical help.

MAGICDRIVE

ON THE SOFT

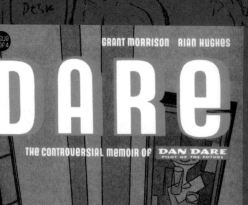

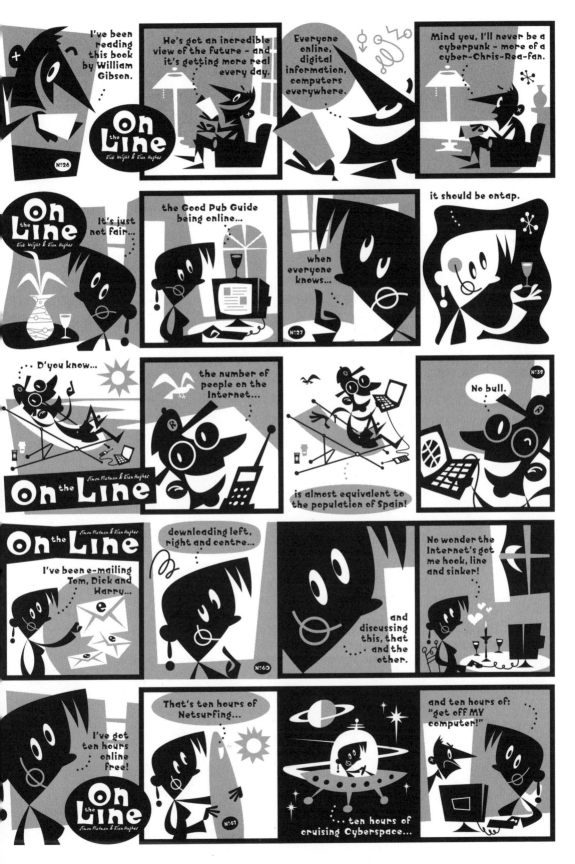

Acton
2000

ABCDEFGHIJKLMNOPQRSTUVWXYZ
abcdefghijklmnopqrstuvwxyzæœ
1234567890

One
One Italic
Two
Two Italic

!!?¿&.,;:...""'',,·»«»«--- __{}{}\/*"'#$£¢¥ƒ%·+=«»@†°¶©®…ÀÈÒÙÁÉÓÚÄËÖÜŸÂÊÔÛÃÑÕÇÅå

Ainsdale
1992

ABCDEFGHIJKLMNOPQRSTUVWXYZ abcdefghijklmnopqrstuvwxyzæœ
1234567890

Medium
Medium Italic
Bold
Bold Italic

!!?¿&.,,... ·"·---··»«»«--- {}{}\/*"'#$£¢¥ƒ%·+=«@†°¶©®…àèòùáéóúäëöüÿâêôûãñõçåø

Amorpheus
1995

ABCDEFGHIJKLMNOPQRSTUVWXYZ
ABCDEFGHIJKLMNOPQRSTUVWXYZœ
1234567890

Regular
Alternates

!!?¿&.,;:...""'',,·»«»«--- _{}{}\/*"'№$£¢¥ƒ%·%+=<>▲†↑®©™ªº ÀÈÒÙÁÉÓÚÄËÖÜŸÂÊÔÛÃÑÕÇÅø

Bingo
1997

ABCDEFGHIJKLMNOPQRSTUVWXYZ
ABCDEFGHIJKLMNOPQRSTUVWXYZ
ÆŒ 1234567890

Regular

!!?¿&.,;:...""'',,·»«»«--- _{}{}\/*"'#$£¢¥ƒ%·%+=«»@†°¶©®™…ÀÈÒÙÁÉÓÚÄËÖÜŸÂÊÔÛÃÑÕÇÅø

Blackcurrant
1997

abcdefghijklmnopqrstuvwxyz
abcdefghijklmnopqrstuvwxyz
æœ 1234567890

Black
Squash
Cameo

!!?¿&.,;:...""'',,·»«»«--- _{}{}\/*"'№$£¢¥ƒ%·%+=«»@†°¶©®™…àèòùáéóúäëöüÿâêôûãñõçåø

Blackcurrant
Alternates
1999

ABCDEFGHIJKLMNOPQRSTUVWXYZ
abcdefghijklmnopqrstuvwxyzæœ
1234567890

Squash Alternates
Black Alternates

!!?¿&.,;:...""'',,·»«»«--- _{}{}\/*"'№$£¢¥ƒ%·%+=«»@†°¶©®™…ÀÈÒÙÁÉÓÚÄËÖÜŸÂÊÔÛÃÑÕÇÅø

Bordello
1997

ABCDEFGHIJKLMNOPQRSTUVWXYZ
abcdefghijklmnopqrstuvwxyzæœfl
1234567890

Bold
Bold Italic
Shaded

!!?¿&.,;:...""'',,·»«»«--- _{}{}\/*"'#$£¢¥ƒ%·%+=«»@†°¶©®™ªºÀÈÒÙÁÉÓÚÄËÖÜŸÂÊÔÛÃÑÕÇÅø

Bullroller
1999

ABCDEFGHIJKLMNOPQRSTUVWXYZ
abcdefghijklmnopqrstuvwxyzææœ
1234567890

Regular

Chantal
1993

ABCDEFGHIJKLMNOPQRSTUVWxYZ
ABCDEFGHIJKLMNOPQRSTUVWxYZ
1234567890

Regular

Chascarillo
1998

ABCDEFGHIJKLMNOPQRSTUVWXYZ
abcdefghijklmnopqrstuvwxyzææœÅ
1234567890

Regular

Citrus
1999

ABCDEFGHIJKLMNOPQRSTUVWXYZ
abcdefghijklmnopqrstuvwxyzœœœ
1234567890

Regular

Cottingley
1993

abcdefghijklmnopqrstuvwxyz
abcdefghijklmnopqrstuvwxyzææœ
1234567890   links l'inks

Regular
Incoming
Outgoing

Cyberdelic
1995

ABCDEFGHIJKLMNOPQRSTUVWXYZ
ABCDEFGHIJKLMNOPQRSTUVWXYZ
1234567890

Regular

Darkside
1993

abcdefghijklmnopqrstuvwxyzææœ
1234567890

Regular
Italic
Bright

Data 90
2002

ABCDEFGHIJKLMNOPQRSTUVWXYZ
ABCDEFGHIJKLMNOPQRSTUVWXYZ
1234567890

Regular
Outline
Shaded

!!?¿&.,:;..""''",.»«‹›«---_OOↃ/™#$£€¥%+=©@†°¶@©°%ÀÈÒÙÁÉÓÚÄËÖÜŸÂÊÔÛÃÑÕÇÅ°

Doom Platoon
1997

ABCDEFGHIJKLMNOPQRSTUVWXYZ
ABCDEFGHIJKLMNOPQRSTUVWXYZ
1234567890

Medium
Bold

!!?¿&.,:;..""''",.»«‹›«---_()⟨⟩⊃⊏⊐\/※#$£¢¥%+=()@†°¶@©°%ÀÈÒÙÁÉÓÚÄËÖÜŸÂÊÔÛÃÑÕÇÅ°

Elektron
1992

ABCDEFGHIJKLMNOPQRSTUVWXYZ
abcdefghijklmnopqrstuvwxyzæœ
1234567890

Light
Medium
Bold
Shaded

!!?¿&.,:;..""''",.»«‹›«---_()-()-()V+""#$£¢¥ƒ°ſ°ſ°º+=©@†°|©@™°ªºÀÈÒÙÁÉÓÚÄËÖÜŸÂÔÛÃÑÕÇÅ°

English Grotesque
1998

ABCDEFGHIJKLMNOPQRSTUVWXYZ
abcdefghijklmnopqrstuvwxyzæœ
1234567890

Thin
Light
Medium
Bold
Extra Bold
Black

!!?¿&.,:;..""''",.»«‹›«---_(){}⊏⊐V/™*""№$£¢¥ƒ%‰+=©@†¶®©™°ªºÀÈÒÙÁÉÓÚÄËÖÜŸÂÊÔÛÃÑÕÇÅøß

Flak
2002

ABCDEFGHIJKLMNOPQRSTUVWXYZ
abcdefghijklmnopqrstuvwxyzæœ
1234567890

Regular
Spraycard
Nailed
Heavy

!!?¿&.,:;..""''",.»«‹›«---_⊏⊐⊐V*""#$£¢¥ƒ%‰•+=©@†¶®©™°°ÀÈÒÙÁÉÓÚÄËÖÜŸÂÊÔÛÃÑÕÇÅøß

Foonky
1995

ABCDEFGHIJKLMNOPQRSTUVWXYZ
abcdefghijklmnopqrstuvwxyzæœ
1234567890

Heavy
Starred

!!?¿&.,:;..""''",.»«‹›«---_⊏⊐⊐V*""№$£¢¥X%.=©@†°¶©@™°ªºÀÈÒÙÁÉÓÚÄËÖÜŸÂÊÔÛÃÑÕÇÅøß

Ragnarok
1992

ABCDEFGHIJKLMNOPQRSTUVWXYZ
abcdefghijklmnopqrstuvwxyz
1234567890

Extra Light
Light
Medium
Bold
Heavy
Outline

!?&.,:;..""''"-⊏⊐"$£¢%

Freeman
2001

Regulr
Italic
Black
Black Italic

ABCDEFGHIJKLMNOPQRSTUVWXYZ
abcdefghijklmnopqrstuvwxyzæœfl
1234567890

Game Over
1999

Regular

ABCDEFGHIJKLMN
OPQRSTUVWXYZÆ
1234567890

Gargoyle
1998

Black
Cameo

ABCDEFGHIJKLMNOPQRSTUVWXYZ 1234567890
abcdefghijklmnopqrstuvwxyzæœfl

Gran Turismo
1998

Regular
Italic
Outline
Shaded

ABCDEFGHIJKLMNOPQRSTUVWXYZ
abcdefghijklmnopqrstuvwxyzæœ
1234567890

**Gran Turismo
Extended**
1998

Regular
Italic

ABCDEFGHIJKLMNOPQRSTUVWXYZ
abcdefghijklmnopqrstuvwxyzæœ
1234567890

Griffin
1997

Black
Italic
Shaded
Dynamo Caps

ABCDEFGHIJKLMNOPQRSTUVWXYZ
abcdefghijklmnopqrstuvwxyzæœ
1234567890

**Haulage
Commercial**
2000

Bold
Bold Italic
Striped
Striped Italic

AABBCCODEEFGGHHIJJKLLMMNOOP
PQQRRSSTTUUVVWWXXYYZZ
1234567890

Jemima
1992

ABCDEFGHIJKLMNOPQRSTUVWXYZ
1234567890
ÆŒ

Regular
Shadow
Italic

!!?¿&.,:;...‘‘‘’’’,,«»‹›‹›‹---_()[]V*™#$€¢¥ƒ%‰+ =÷©†°↑®©™△▲ÀÉÙÀÉÒÙÀÉÒÙÀÉÒÙÀÑÕÇÅø

Judgement
1997

ABCDEFGHIJKLMNOPQRSTUVWXYZ
ABCDEFGHIJKLMNOPQRSTUVWXYZÆŒ
1234567890

Black
Black Italic
Bold
Bold Italic
Medium
Medium Italic

!!?¿&.,:;...‘‘‘’’’,,«»‹›‹›‹---()[]V*™№$€¢¥ƒ%₀%₀₀=÷@†°¶®©™₀₀ÀÊÙÀÉÒÙÀÉÒÙÑÕÇÅø

**Judgement
Condensed**
1997

ABCDEFGHIJKLMNOPQRSTUVWXYZ
ABCDEFGHIJKLMNOPQRSTUVWXYZÆŒ
1234567890

Black
Black Italic

!!?¿&.,:;...‘‘‘’’’,,«»‹›‹›‹---()[]V*™№$€¢¥ƒ%₀%₀₀+=÷@†°¶®©™₀₀ÀÉÙÀÉÒÙÀÉÒÙÀÉÒÙÑÕÇÅø

**Judgement
Compressed**
1997

ABCDEFGHIJKLMNOPQRSTUVWXYZ
ABCDEFGHIJKLMNOPQRSTUVWXYZÆŒ
1234567890

Regular
Italic
Inline

!!?¿&...‘‘‘’’’,,«»‹›---()[]V*™™№$€¢¥₀+=÷@†°¶®©™₀₀ÀÉÒÙÀÉÒÙÀÉÒÙÑÕÇÅø

**Judgement
Decoratives**
1997

ABCDEFGHIJKLMNOPQRSTUVWXYZ
ABCDEFGHIJKLMNOPQRSTUVWXYZÆŒ
1234567890

Stencil
Stencil Italic
Highlight
Embossed
Rimmed
Shadow

!!?¿&.,:;...‘‘‘’’’,,«»‹›‹›‹---()[]V*™№$€¢¥ƒ%₀%₀₀+=÷@†°¶®©™₀₀ÀÉÙÀÉÒÙÀÉÒÙÀÉÒÙÑÕÇÅø

Hounslow
1998

ABCDEFGHIJKLMNOPQRSTUVWXYZ
ABCDEFGHIJKLMNOPQRSTUVWXYZÆŒ
1234567890

Solid
Shadow
Open
Sold Italic
Open Italic
Shadow Italic

!!?¿&.,:;...‘‘‘’’’,,«»‹›‹---_()[]V*™#$€¢¥ƒ ₀₀+=÷@†°¶®©™₀₀ÀÉÙÀÉÒÙÀÉÒÙÀÉÒÙÑÕÇÅø

Jakita Wide
2000

ABCDEFGHIJKLMNOPQRSTUVWXYZ
abcdefghijklmnopqrstuvwxyzæœ
1234567890

Regular
Bold
Inline

!!?¿&.,:;...‘‘‘’’’,,«»‹›---_()[]V*™#$€¢¥ƒ%₀%₀₀+=÷@†°¶®©™₀₀ÀÉÙÀÉÒÙÀÉÒÙÀÉÒÙÑÕÇÅø

Laydeez Nite
1997

ABCDEFGHIJKLMNOPQRSTUVWXYZ
ABCDEFGHIJKLMNOPQRSTUVWXYZÆŒ
1234567890

Regular

Lusta
1997

ABCDEFGHIJKLMNOPQRSTUVWXYZ 1234567890

abcdefghijklmnopqrstuvwxyzææoe

Forty Sans
Eighty Sans
Forty Serif
Eighty Serif
One Twenty Sans
One Sixty Sans
Two Hundred Sans

Mastertext
1993

ABCDEFGHIJKLMNOPQRSTUVWXYZ
ABCDEFGHIJKLMNOPQRSTUVWXYZÆŒ
1234567890

Light
Plain
Heavy
Boxed

Metropol Noir
1995

ABCDEFGHIJKLMNOPQRSTUVWXYZ
ABCDEFGHIJKLMNOPQRSTUVWXYZÆŒ
1234567890

Regular

Mystique
2000

ABCDEFGHIJKLMNOPQRSTUVWXYZ
ABCDEFGHIJKLMNOPQRSTUVWXYZ
1234567890

Blaque
Fantasie
Cosmique

Novak
2000

ABCDEFGHIJKLMNOPQRSTUVWXYZ
abcdefghijklmnopqrstuvwxyz*.
1234567890

Winter
Spring

Paralucent
2000

ABCDEFGHIJKLMNOPQRSTUVWXYZ
abcdefghijklmnopqrstuvwxyzæœfl
1234567890

Thin
Extra Light
Light
Medium
Demi Bold
Bold
Heavy

Paralucent Italic
2000

Thin Italic
Extra Light Italic
Light Italic
Medium Italic
Demi Bold Italic
Bold Italic
Heavy Italic

ABCDEFGHIJKLMNOPQRSTUVWXYZ
abcdefghijklmnopqrstuvwxyzæœefl
1234567890

Paralucent Condensed
2001

Thin
Extra Light
Light
Medium
Demi Bold
Bold
Heavy

ABCDEFGHIJKLMNOPQRSTUVWXYZ
abcdefghijklmnopqrstuvwxyzæœefl
1234567890

Paralucent Condensed Italic
2001

Thin Italic
Extra Light Italic
Light Italic
Medium Italic
Demi Bold Italic
Bold Italic
Heavy Italic

ABCDEFGHIJKLMNOPQRSTUVWXYZ
abcdefghijklmnopqrstuvwxyzæœefl
1234567890

Platinum
2000

Regular
Inline

ABCDEFGHIJKLMNOPQRSTUVWXYZ
abcdefghijklmnopqrstuvwxyzæœefl
1234567890

Quagmire
1997

Medium
Demi
Bold
Black

ABCDEFGHIJKLMNOPQRSTUVWXYZ
abcdefghijklmnopqrstuvwxyzæœefl
1234567890

Quagmire Italic
1997

Medium Italic
Demi Italic
Bold Italic
Black Italic

ABCDEFGHIJKLMNOPQRSTUVWXYZ
abcdefghijklmnopqrstuvwxyzæœefl
1234567890

Quagmire Extended
1997

Medium
Bold

ABCDEFGHIJKLMNOPQRSTUVWXYZ
abcdefghijklmnopqrstuvwxyzæœefl
1234567890

Quagmire Extended Italic
1997

ABCDEFGHIJKLMNOPQRSTUVWXYZ
abcdefghijklmnopqrstuvwxyzæœfl
1234567890

Medium
Bold

!!?¿&.,:;..'''',.«»‹›<---()[]{}\/‡\#$£¢¥ƒº₀ºº₀₀+=÷→@†º¹®©™ªºÅÈÒÙÁÉÓÚÄËÖÜÿÂÊÔÛÃÑÕÇÅø

Range
2000

ABCDEFGHIJKLMNOPQRSTUVWXYZ
abcdefghijklmnopqrstuvwxyzœæ
1234567890

Light
Medium
Bold
Extra Bold
Black

!!?¿&.,:;..''''',.«»‹›<---()[]{}\/*"#$£¢¥ƒ%‰.=÷@°¹®©™ªºÀÈÒÙÁÉÓÚÄËÖÔÛÃÑÕÇÅø

Reasonist
1992

ABCDEFGHIJKLMNOPQRSTUVWXYZ
ABCDEFGHIJKLMNOPQRSTUVWXYZÆŒ
1234567890

Medium
Medium Italic

!!?¿&.,:;..'''',.«»‹›<---()[]{}\/|''''º¢$£¢¥%₊=÷.^†¶©ªºÀÈÒÙÁÉÓÚÄËÖÜÿÂÊÔÛÃÑÕÇÅø

Register
2000

ABCDEFGHIJKLMNOPQRSTUVWXYZ
abcdefghijklmnopqrstuvwxyzæœfl
1234567890

Extra Light
Light
Medium
Demi Bold
Bold

!!?¿&.,:;..'''',.»«‹›<---_()[]{}\/*"#$£¢¥ƒ%₀‰+=÷→@†º¹®©™ªºÀÈÒÙÁÉÓÚÄËÖÜÿÂÔÛÃÑÕÇÅø

Register Italic
2000

ABCDEFGHIJKLMNOPQRSTUVWXYZ
abcdefghijklmnopqrstuvwxyzœœfl
1234567890

Extra Light Italic
Light Italic
Medium Italic
Demi Bold Italic
Bold Italic

!!?¿&..:;.. """,,«»‹›<---_()[]{}\/*"#$£¢¥ƒ%‰+=÷→@†º¹®©™ªºÀÈÒÙÁÉÓÚÄËÖÜÿÂÔÛÃÑÕÇÅø

Register Wide
2000

ABCDEFGHIJKLMNOPQRSTUVWXYZ
abcdefghijklmnopqrstuvwxyzæœfl
1234567890

Extra Light
Light
Medium
Demi Bold
Bold

!!?¿&..:;.. """,,.»«‹›<---_()[]{}\/*"#$£¢¥ƒ%₀‰+=÷→@†º¹®©™ªºÀÈÒÙÁÉÓÚÄËÖÜÿÂÔÛÃÑÕÇÅø

Register Wide Italic
2000

ABCDEFGHIJKLMNOPQRSTUVWXYZ
abcdefghijklmnopqrstuvwxyzœœfl
1234567890

Extra Light Italic
Light Italic
Medium Italic
Demi Bold Italic
Bold Italic

!!?¿&..:;.. """,,.»«‹›<---_()[]{}\/*"#$£¢¥ƒ%₀‰+=÷→@†º¹®©™ªºÀÈÒÙÁÉÓÚÄËÖÜÿÂÔÛÃÑÕÇÅø

Register Condensed 2000

ABCDEFGHIJKLMNOPQRSTUVWXYZ
abcdefghijklmnopqrstuvwxyzæœfl
1234567890

Bold
Bold Italic

!¡?¿&.,:;..""'',,·»«()‹---_[]{}|\/*''#\$£¢¥f%‰+=‹›@†°¶®©™ªºÀÈÒÙÁÉÓÚÄËÖÜŸÂÊÔÛÃÑÕÇÅø

Regulator 1992

ABCDEFGHIJKLMNOPQRSTUVWXYZ
abcdefghijklmnopqrstuvwxyzæœ
1234567890

Thin
Light
Medium
Bold
Heavy
Cameo

!¡?¿&.,:;..""'',,·»«()‹---O[]{}|\/*''''Nº\$£¢¥f%‰+=‹›ªT†°¶®©™ªºÀÈÒÙÁÉÓÚÄËÖÜŸÂÊÔÛÃÑÕÇÅØ§

Regulator Italic 1993

ABCDEFGHIJKLMNOPQRSTUVWXYZ
abcdefghijklmnopqrstuvwxyzæœ
1234567890

Thin Italic
Light Italic
Medium Italic
Bold Italic
Heavy Italic

!¡?¿&.,:;.. ''',,·»«X---O[]{}|\/*''''Nº\$£¢¥f%‰+=‹›ªT†°¶®©™ªºÀÈÒÙÁÉÓÚÄEÖUŸÂÊÔÛÃÑÕÇÅØ§

Ritafurey 1992

ABCDEFGHIJKLMNOPQRSTUVWXYZ
abcdefghijklmnopqrstuvwxyzæœ
1234567890

Bold
Bold Italic

!¡?¿&.,:;..""'''',,·»«()‹---O[]{}|\/*''#\$£¢¥f%‰+=‹→@†°¶®©™ªºÀÈÒÙÁÉÓÚÄËÖÜŸÂÊÔÛÃÑÕÇÅø

Scrotnig 1995

ABCDEFGHIJKLMNOPQRSTUVWXYZ
abcdefghijklmnopqrstuvwxyz
1234567890

Medium
Heavy

!¡?¿&.,:;..""''",,·→◄◄►---OOOU''''®\$£¢¥f%‰+=-·@†°¶®©™ªºàèòùáéóúäëöüÿâêôûãñõçàø

Scrotnig Condensed 1996

ABCDEFGHIJKLMNOPQRSTUVW
XYZÆŒ 1234567890

Condensed
Condensed Italic

!¡?¿&.,:;..""''",,·►►◄◄►---OOOU''''®\$£¢¥f%‰+·-@†°¶®©™ªºàèòùáéóúäëöüÿâêôûãñõçàø

September 2001

ABCDEFGHIJKLMNOPQRSTUVWXYZ
abcdefghijklmnopqrstuvwxyzæœfl
1234567890

Medium
Medium Italic
Bold
Bold Italic

!¡?¿&.,:;..""''",,·»«()‹---O[]{}|\/*''#\$£¢¥f%‰+=‹›@†°¶®©™ªºÀÈÒÙÁÉÓÚÄËÖÜŸÂÊÔÛÃÑÕÇÅØ§

Skylab
2001

ABCDEFGHIJKLMNOPQRSTUVWXYZ
ABCDEFGHIJKLMNOPQRSTUVWXYZ
1234567890

Regular
Capsule
Code

Slack Casual
1993

ABCDEFGHIJKLMNOPQRSTUVWXYZ abcdefghijklmnopqrstuvwxyzæø
1234567890

Medium
Medium Italic
Bold
Bold Italic

Space Cadet
1995

ABCDEFGHIJKLMNOPQRSTUVWXYZ
1234567890

Regular

Stadia
1996

ABCDEFGHIJKLMNOPQRSTUVWXYZ
abcdefghijklmnopqrstuvwxyzæø
1234567890°

Regular
Outline

Silesia
1993

ABCDEFGHIJKLMNOPQRSTUVWXYZ
abcdefghijklmnopqrstuvwxyzæø
1234567890

Thin
Light
Medium
Bold
Heavy
Inline

Sinclair Display
2000

ABCDEFGHIJKLMNOPQRSTUVWXYZ
abcdefghijklmnopqrstuvwxyzæøfl
1234567890

Regular

Sinclair Biform
2000

ABCDEFGHIJKLMNOPQRSTUVWXYZ
abcdefghijklmnopqrstuvwxyzæøfl
1234567890

Regular

Substation 2002
Regular

Telecast 1996
Regular
Spare Parts

Terrazzo 1997
Regular

Transmat 1997
Regular
Terminals

Untitled One 1994
Regular

ABCDEFGHIJKLMNOPQRSTUVWXYZ
ÆŒ 1234567890

Vertex 1999
Light
Medium
Demi Bold
Bold
Inline
1234567890

Westway 2002
Regular

Wexford Oakley
1998

ABCDEFGHIJKLMNOPQRSTUVWXYZ
abcdefghijklmnopqrstuvwxyzæœfl
1234567890

Regular
Alternates

!?¿&.,:;...""''",,•»«‹---_()[]\/*"#$£€¥%‰+=◊∞@†¶®©ƏƆÀÇȨ̀ÙÀȨ́ÊÀȨ̀ÉÙÀÔÙÃŅ̃ÇÅÆẞ

Zinger
2000

ABCDEFGHIJKLMNOPQRS
TUVWXYZabcdefghijkl
mnopqrstuvwxyzœœ
1234567890

Regular
Italic

Cannon Black | 2" phototypositor negative | c1980

Anytime Now
1997

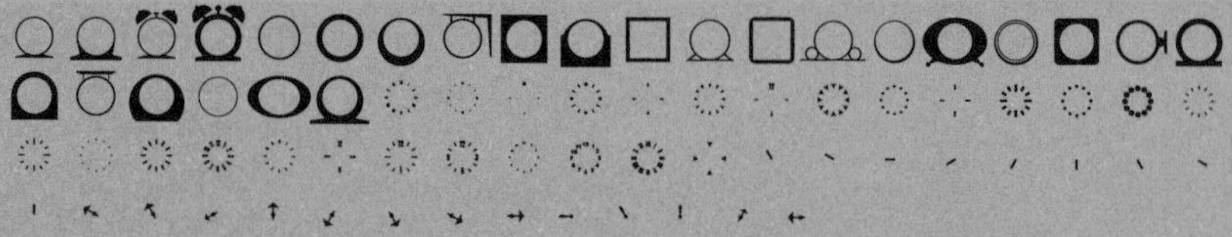

Iconics 1-4
1999

Autofont
1997

Judgement
Icons
1997

NEW
THRILL

Mac Dings
1995

Mastertext
Symbols One
1994

Mastertext
Symbols Two
1994

Menswear
1998

Motorcity
1993

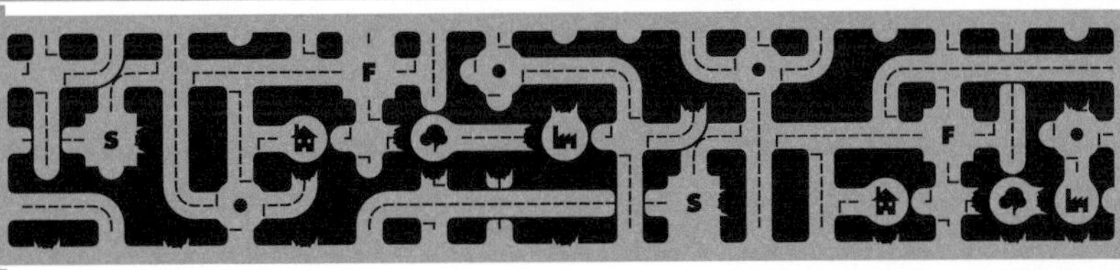

Pic Format
1994

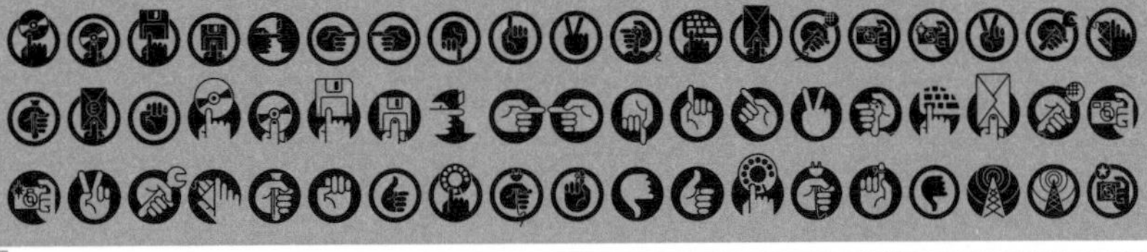

Scrotnig
Hexes One
1993

Scrotnig
Hexes Two
1993

Why Two Kay
1999

Hot Rod
2001

Contour
1992

Regular
Italic
Outline
Shaded

ABCDEFGHIJKLMNOPQRST
UVWXYZÆŒ 1234567890
⊞Ӂ♁Φ♈♍♐♑

Crash Bang Wallop
1989

Light
Light Italic
Medium
Medium Italic
Contoured
Highlight

ABCDEFGHIJKLMNOPQRSTUVWXYZ
abcdefghijklmnopqrstuvwxyzæœ
1234567890

Identification
1993

01
02 Morse
03 Frequency
04 Semaphore
05 Character

1234567890

Knobcheese
1992

Normal
Outline
Initials

ABCDEFGHIJKLMNOPQRSTUVWXYZ
abcdefghijklmnopqrstuvwxyzæœ
1234567890

Outlander
1993

Light
Medium
Bold
Black
White
Binary

ABCDEFGHIJKLMNOPQRSTUVWXYZ
ABCDEFGHIJKLMNOPQRSTUVWXYZ
1234567890

Revolver
1990

Regular
Recoil

ABCDEFGHIJKLMNOPQRSTUVWXYZ
ÆŒ 1234567890

Rian's Dingbats
1993

One
Two
Three
Four

218 | **Guy Ornadel** | Licensed to Thrill | Transient | *CD album* | 1999 |

219 | **Guy Ornadel** | Licensed to Thrill | Transient | *poster* | 1999
| design and art direction: Rian Hughes | photograph: John R. Ward

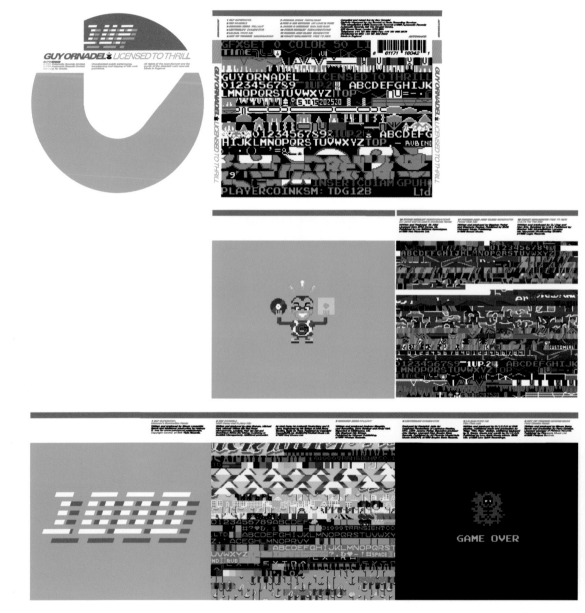

GUYORNADEL
LICENSED TO THRILL

EVERYONE GET READY

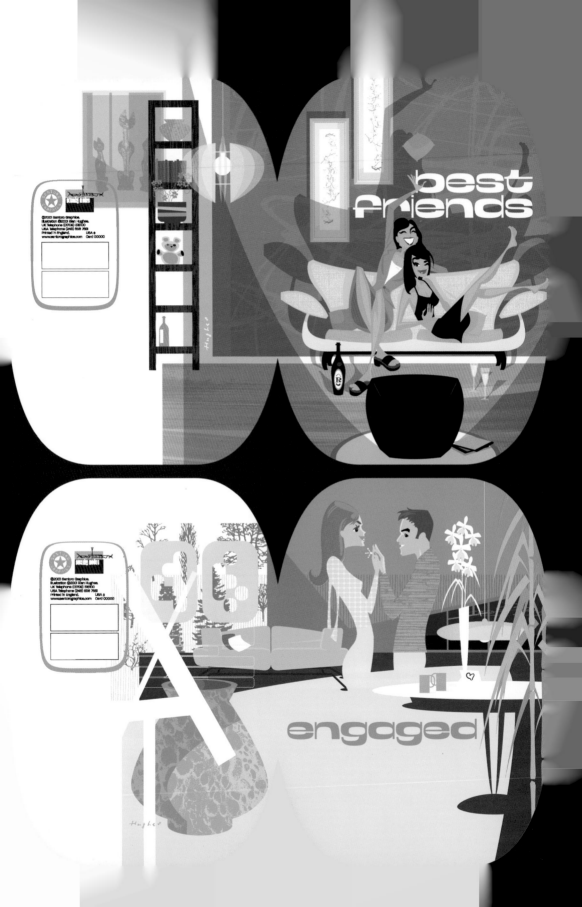

| **hb** | T-shirt | *logo* | 1999 | 229

Reader awards | SFX magazine | *editorial illustration* | 1999 |
Drawing packages | Mac User magazine | *editorial illustration* | 1997 |
Goring Windows | Alan Hughes House | *stained glass windows* | 1999 |
The man who... | Mac User magazine | *editorial illustrations* | 1996 |
You're a Megastar! | Mega magazine | *editorial illustration* | 1997 |
Annotated body | 19 magazine | *editorial illustration* | 2001 |
Just us | You and Your Wedding magazine | *editorial illustration* | 2000 |
Meet the staff | PC Format magazine | *editorial illustration* | 1995 |
Coffee makers | Stuff magazine | *editorial illustration* | 2000 |
Scorch | Bad Boys Inc | A&M Records | *band mascot* | 1993 |
Cyclone Powers | Electrolux / BMB | *promotional illustration* | 1999 |

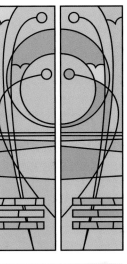

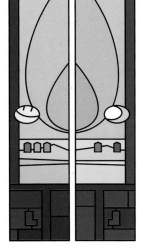

pattern in your head. Sort of, you know, a huge mathematical mantra.

| **Vaio** | Sony / Banner | *brochure illustration (one of twelve)* | 2000 |
| **Which? Car** | Which? magazine | *supplement illustrations (three of twelve)* | 1999
| **Man or Wuss?** | Maxim magazine (US) | *editorial illustration* | 1998
| **How to get Mom off the phone** | Maxim magazine (US) | *editorial illustration* | 1997
| **Aldous Huxley** | Radio Times | *editorial illustration* | 1996
| **Hoaxing the UFO investigators** | Radio Times | *editorial illustration* | 1996
| **Home widescreen cinema** | Ariel magazine (BBC) | *editorial illustration* | 1997
| **Site of Sound** | Brighton Festival website | *animated characters (smoker unused)* | 2000
| **New carriers, new rules** | Communications International magazine | *cover illustration* | 2

TRANR529LP EFA 69629-1 Made in Germany

6 61171 26291 0

8

Transient←8
BACK WITH THE **FUTURE**

240 | **Radio / TV / Tosh / Games / Videos / Anime / Events / Comics / New Media / Toys and Models / CDs / Mail Order / Film / Books**
| SFX magazine | *section headers* | 1995-6
| **Lost episodes**
| SFX magazine | *editorial illustration* | 1998

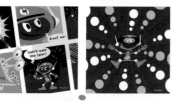

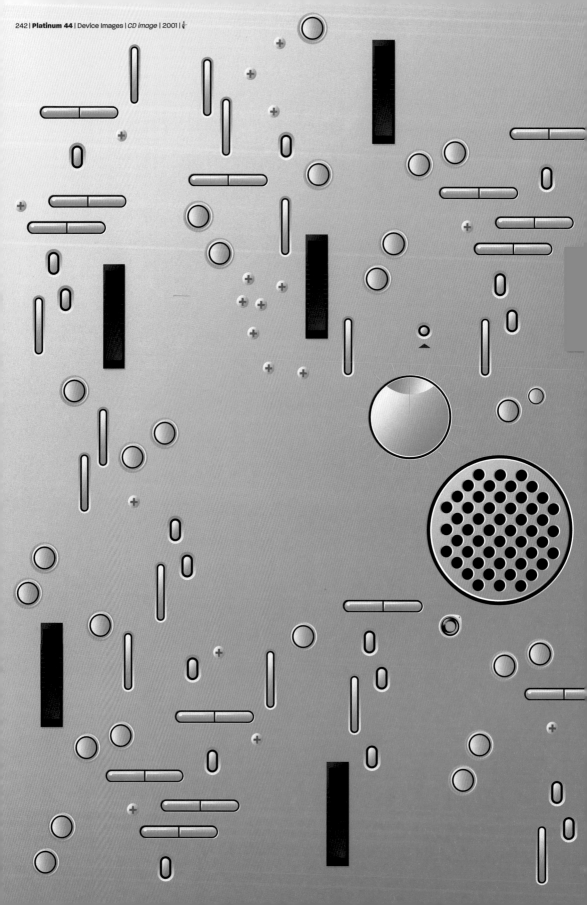

XTC DRUMS AND WIRELESS

BBC Radio Sessions 77-89

TRANSIENT DAWN

music from djset | cosmosis | astral projection | simon posford & chris deckker | slide | cosmix & kristian | medicine drum | messiah
catalogue number transit07cd
release June '07

👤 | **Transient Dawn** | Transient | *poster* | 1997 | 248

Transient Dawn | Transient | *CD album* | 1997 | 249
Transient 4 | Transient | *CD album (interior)* | 1996 |
Transient 4 | Transient | *LP album* | 1996 |

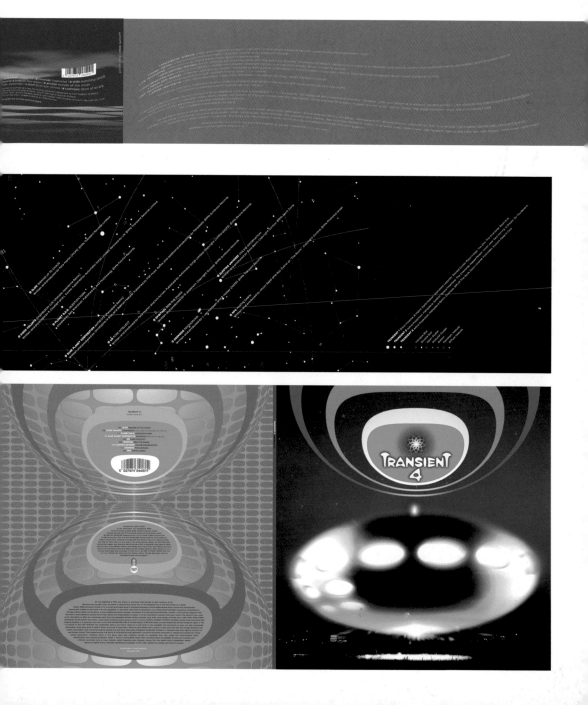

🚶 | **Caped Crusader Classics!** | Bob Kane and various | Titan Books | *paperback book covers* | 1989 | 251
design and art direction: Rian Hughes, 5 and 6 with Carol Thomas and Nigel Davies | illustrations: Bob Kane (ghosted?) |
Love and Rockets | Jaime Hernandez | Titan Books | *graphic novel cover* | 1987 |
design and art direction: Rian Hughes | illustration: Jaime Hernandez |
Ape Sex | Jaime Hernandez | Titan Books | *graphic novel cover* | 1989 |
design and art direction: Rian Hughes | illustration: Jaime Hernandez |
Mechanix | Jaime Hernandez | Titan Books | *graphic novel cover* | 1988 |
design and art direction: Rian Hughes | illustration: Jaime Hernandez |
Human Diastrophism | Gilbert Hernandez | Titan Books | *graphic novel cover* | 1989 |
design and art direction: Rian Hughes | illustration: Gilbert Hernandez |

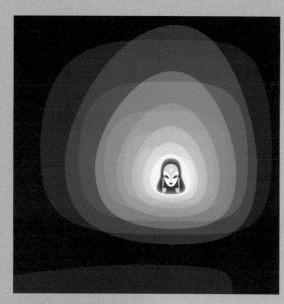

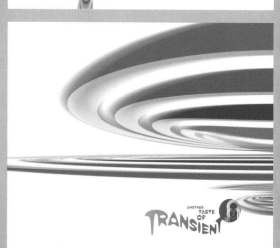

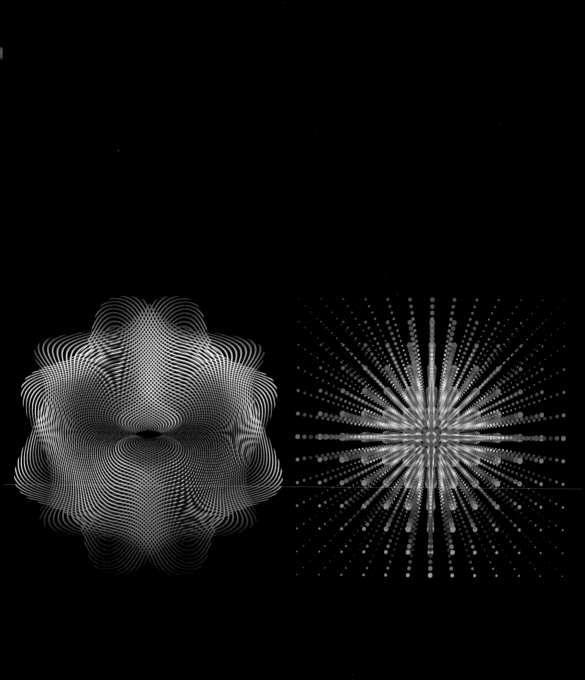

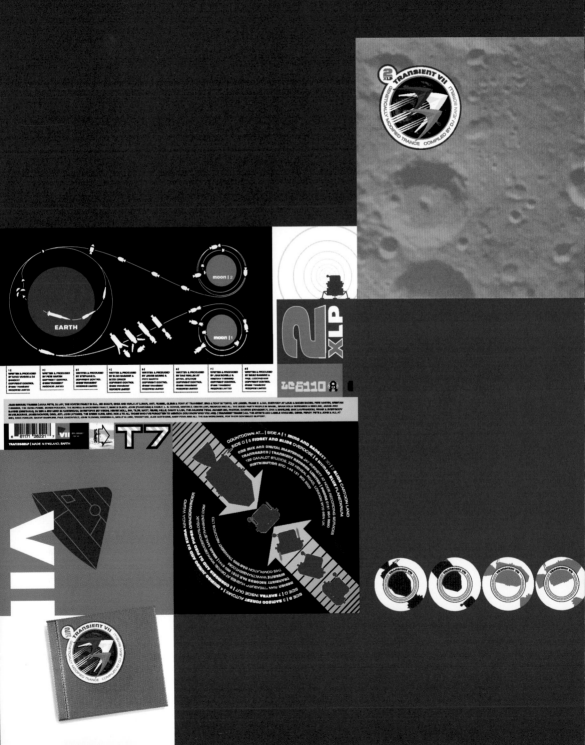

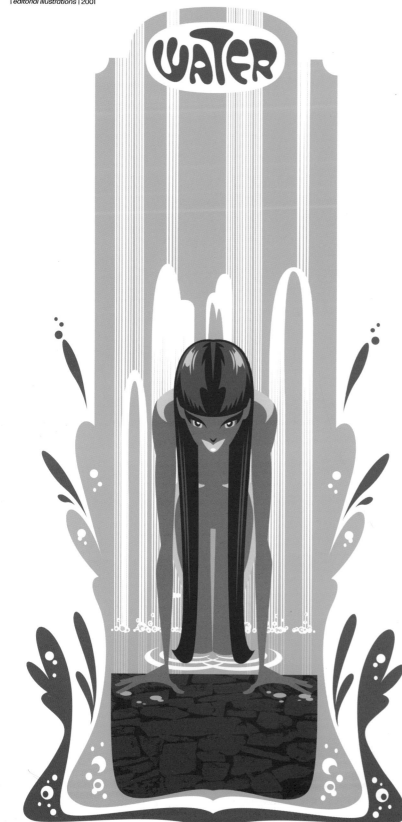

New Pad | *greeting card (unpublished)* | 1999 | 261
Ultra Louche | Idée Fixe | *greeting card* | 1996 |

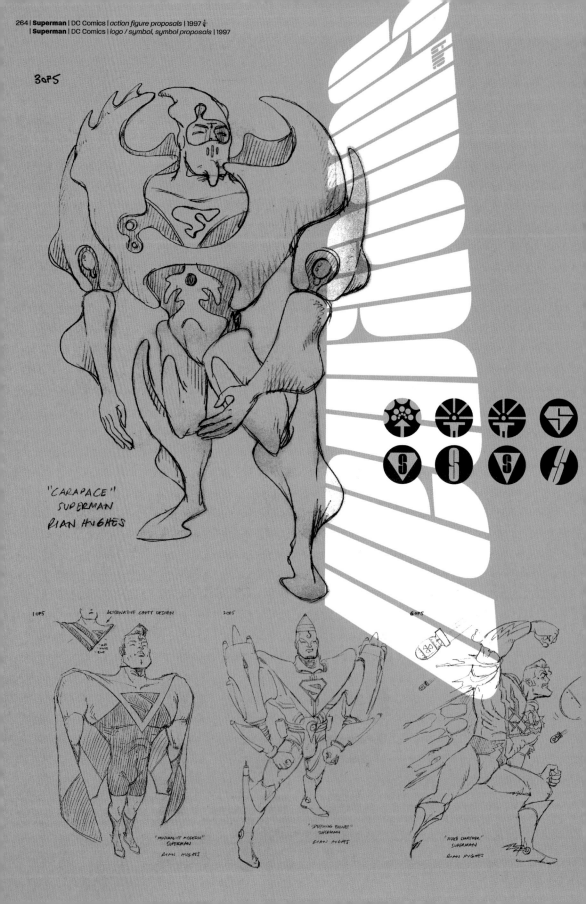

3 of 5

"CARAPACE"
SUPERMAN
RIAN HUGHES

1 of 5   ALTERNATIVE CHEST DESIGN

"MINIMALIST MODERN"
SUPERMAN
RIAN HUGHES

2 of 5

"SPEEDING BULLET"
SUPERMAN
RIAN HUGHES

6 of 5

"NUKE CRASHER"
SUPERMAN
RIAN HUGHES

🕯 | **The Inheritors** | Modern Era Editions | *graphic novel* | design and illustration: Rian Hughes | writer: Rian Hughes | 1988 | **The Science Service** | Atomium 58 editions | 265
Magic Strip / Acme Comics | *graphic novel* | 1987 | design and illustration: Rian Hughes | writer: Rian Hughes / John Freeman | **Raymond Chandler: Goldfish** | Byron Preiss |
graphic novel (unpublished) | 1992 | design and illustration: Rian Hughes | writer: Raymond Chandler, adapted by Tom DeHaven | **Really and Truly** | 2000AD | cover (inset) |
comic series | 1993 | Illustration: Rian Hughes | writer: Grant Morrison | **The Science Service** | Atomium 58 editions | Magic Strip / Acme Comics | *graphic novel (interior pages)* |
1987 | design and illustration: Rian Hughes | writers: Rian Hughes / John Freeman | **Robohunter** | 2000AD | *comic series* | 1994 | Illustration: Rian Hughes | writer: Peter Hogan |
Really and Truly | 2000AD | cover | *comic series* | 1993 | Illustration: Rian Hughes | writer: Grant Morrison | **Really and Truly** | 2000AD | *comic series* | 1993 |
Illustration: Rian Hughes | writer: Grant Morrison | **Mean 16** | 2000AD | cover | *comic series* | 1993 | **The Lighted Cities** | Fox comics | *comic strip* | 1989 | Illustration: Rian Hughes |
writer: Chris Reynolds | **Visions of the Future** | *card series* | 1993 | *with pre-digital colour separation overlay* | **Spiffy Designs** | *cards and gum collection* | 1989 |

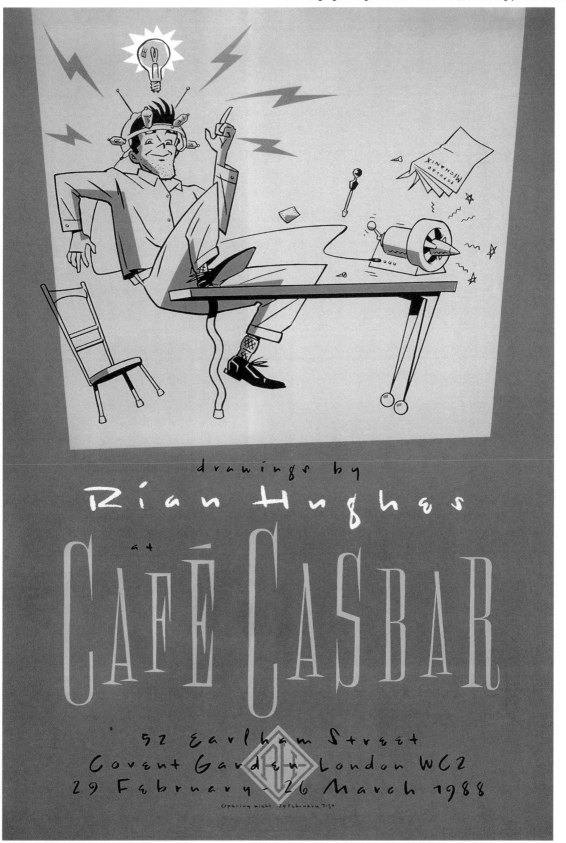

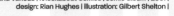

Xpresso | Fleetway | *magazine cover* | 1991 | design and art direction: Rian Hughes | illustration: Milo Manara | |
| **Xpresso** | Fleetway | *magazine introduction page* | 1991 | design and art direction: Rian Hughes | illustration: Rian Hughes
| **Revolver** | Fleetway | *magazine covers* | 1991 | design and art direction: Rian Hughes | illustrations: Rian Hughes | Brendan McCarthy | Steve Parkhouse
| **Xpresso** | Fleetway | *magazine spreads* | 1991 | design: Rian Hughes | illustrations: Rian Hughes
| **The Revolver Romance Special** | Fleetway | *magazine contents spread* | 1991 | design: Rian Hughes | illustration: Rian Hughes
| **Bring Me Your Love** | Fleetway | *magazine page* | 1991 | design: Rian Hughes | illustration: Robert Crumb
| **The Revolver Romance Special** | Fleetway | *magazine cover* | 1991 | design: Rian Hughes | illustration: Brian Bolland
| **Heart Throbs** | Max Cabanes | Fleetway | *graphic novel* | 1991 | design: Rian Hughes | illustration: Max Cabanes
| **Hewligan's Haircut** | Pete Milligan and Jamie Hewlett | Fleetway | *graphic novel* | 1991 | design and art direction: Rian Hughes | illustration: Jamie Hewlett | photography: John R. Ward

| **Speakeasy** | John Brown Publishing | *magazine* | 1990-2 | design and art direction: Rian Hughes | illustrations: Rian Hughes | Dave Gibbons | Jamie Hewlett | Charles Burns | 271

Aliens | Dark Horse (UK) | *magazine* | 1992 | design and art direction: Rian Hughes | illustrations: Kelley Jones |

Judge Dredd: Def Eds | Fleetway | *graphic novels* | 1990 | design and art direction: Rian Hughes | illustrations: William Maher | Brendan McCarthy | Fastner and Larson |

Soda | Fleetway | *magazine proposal* | 1990 | design and art direction: Rian Hughes | main illustration: Franquin |

Revolver | Fleetway | *contents page* | 1991 | design and art direction: Rian Hughes | illustration: Rian Hughes |

Sam Bronx and the Robots | Serge Clerc | Acme Comics | *graphic novel* | 1991 | design and art direction: Rian Hughes | illustration: Serge Clerc |

| design and art direction: Rian Hughes | cover illustrations: issues 1, 2, 4, 6, 7, 9, 12 Carlos Ezquerra | 13, 22, 26, 40 Glenn Fabry | 20 Brendan McCarthy | 23, 27, 30, 34, 52 Sean Phillips | 29 Warren Pleece | 45 Dave Hine | 51 Paul Johnson | 53, 58 Dix | 55 José Munoz | 57 David Vallely | 59 Steve Samson | 60, 63 Milo Manara | 61 Gary Erskine

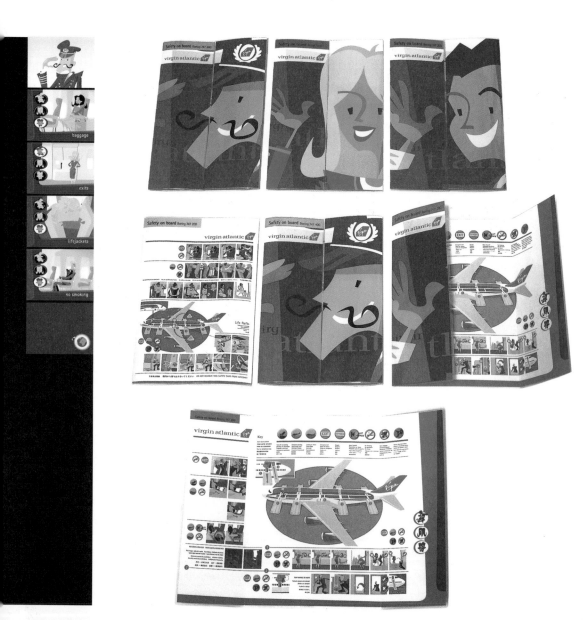

The best photograph I didn't take:

Place: Lima, Peru. Date: 1996. Scene: an old covered market. Between a stall selling nothing but fridge magnets and another selling second-hand radio parts is a stall stacked with pyramids of rolled-up posters. Pinned above are three examples. Why these three? Do they illustrate the range available? Are they simply the best sellers? The three posters are, left to right: A '70s soft-focus photograph of a loaf of bread, wheat and a glass of milk on a wooden tabletop. A sumptuous reproduction of an old painting of Mary cradling the infant Jesus, all rich maroons and golds. And lastly Arnie as the Terminator: black leathers, shades, and uzis coughing fire. Is this the aspirational holy trinity? Food, religion, and... Arnie.

Commentary

Rian Hughes

| 12-13 | **Psybadek** | Look closely – the condom wrappers actually contain decks. A perforated sheet (of roaches?) is used as a promotional magazine insert. The game packaging itself is here signed by David Holmes. The studio unfortunately doesn't own a pristine one.

| 16-17 | **La Linea: London's Latin Music Festival** | Complimentary colourways for two successive years of this popular festival. Art directed by John Pasche.

| 18 | **Saturday Night Fever** | For those with good eyesight and a magnifying glass, our heroine is wearing *Wombles*, *Look-in* and *Blue Peter* badges.

| 18-19, 21 | **Yellow Boots** | The characters featured in these seasonal posters are wearing clothes actually available in the store. Cerise fur-edged PVC, anyone?

| 20 | **Forbidden Planet** | This logo evokes the sf optimism of the NASA logo and the TV-shaped futurism of Adrian Frutiger's Microgramma, remembered from the livery of the Shado Mobiles from Gerry Anderson's TV series *UFO*. This design presaged the resurgence in popularity of the extended font. The shop is affectionately known as FP in comic and sf circles.

| 22-24 | **Jet Set Radio Future** | The background image features graffiti shot around the Westway near Paddington in London, close to the studio.

| 31 | **Tyro Typo** | A late-night beer-fuelled kerning session. Not recommended.

| 33 | **Transient 2** | Goa-inspired imagery for this trance label's regular compilation series.

| 34 | **Birthday Girl** | The cards that inspired a few "homages"...

| 35 | **Storecard credit** | Because only 40% of communication is verbal. The rest says "materialistic sucker".

| 36 | **Telica** | Sleeve for UK-based Italian house outfit, featuring a propellor and a sprinkling of updated dynamo futurista.

| 38 | **The Animalhouse** | Japanese release only.

| 40 | **Miss Wong** | The art establishment will finally come around and I will live to see the Trechikoff retrospective at the Tate Modern be the most popular show they have ever put on.

| 44-47 | **Annotated Bodies** | The icons refer the reader to a series of box-out descriptions detailing the body's responses to this month's situation.

| 48 | **Cocaine's route to clubland** | I got paid in money for this one.

| 49 | **How often do women think about sex?** | Not as often as *Maxim* readers.

| 49 | **Shagometer** | *More!* magazine readers, on the other hand...

| 49 | **Self promotion for graduates** | Graduates have to promote themselves by any means to get a job. Calling cards advertising O and A levels in phone boxes might be one way. Unfortunately the Manufacturing, Science and Finance Worker's Union (MSF) disagreed. The magazine did, however, reprint articles and illustrations without permission, something most capitalist magazines ceased to do fifteen years ago. Up the workers!

| 50 | **Razor's Edge: Exquisite Sin** | The Exquisite Sin fetish icon shows what too much clubbing can do to you. Shiny and new to old and knackered in four stages. These images ran over the four labels on the vinyl double album.

| 51 | **Transient 3** | More spiritual Goa-style trance from Transient. The buddha image was actually taken in Thailand.

| 52 | **John '00' Fleming** | A confluence of John's punning name and high-tech DJ paraphernalia. The transparent record box houses a bomb while attacking 12" UFOs come in for the kill. The inset logo features a Technics deck with telescopic sight crosshairs. Small inset: Secret revealed – John lying on his side in an unretouched polaroid.

| 54 | **Monique de Roissy** | Steven Cook is an artist who works with digital media and photography. His *Alternity* series manifests possible pasts in startlingly believable photographic images. .

| 55 | **Geri Halliwell** | Ginger Spice winks at us on the back cover – an idea reused from Transient 2. The image was foil blocked onto matt white card stock. Art directed by Rob O'Connor.

| 58 | **Angels Unlimited** | Shown as silver here, the cover lettering originally featured a shimmery blocked holofoil.

| 59 | **Letters to Liz** | Photo-booth images of each book's two main protagonists in a variety of settings – pinboard, fridge... The "photographs" are illustrated, whereas the other images are all photographic.

| 62 | **Visitors from Oz** | The lettering on this book was originally skyscraper-vertical. Conceptually sound but not marketing department friendly.

| 62 | **The Secret Paris of the 1930s** | Unpublished college project. Transparent negative dustjacket over an image taken from an old style glass-plate camera back.

| 63 | **Room with a View** | English and Italian, reserve versus expression.

| 64 | **Street Scents** | These posters, which ran throughout the world with the exception of the UK, were printed in one large batch and then overprinted locally using Citrus, a specially commissioned font. This led to many interesting word placements, some obscuring faces entirely. The Koreans asked for the green devil girl to be topped and tailed and swapped in the foreground with the less controversial yellow character, while in the Middle East they were all asked to cover up any bare flesh.

| 66 | **Tranceformer** | Technotribal head montaged from a variety of modern motorcycle parts.

| 69 | **Fiell** | Peter Fiell, proprietor and author, asked for something evoking classic international airplane travel.

| 72-73, 76-77, 80-81 | **Cringe** | *New Woman* readers share their most embarrassing moments.

| 74, 75 | **Friends Forever** | To achieve a rough-edged texture, these figures were drawn on toilet paper and then scanned.

| 82 | **Eve** | Hardcore but uplifting dance label. The glass and steel inset images are taken from the CNBDI in Angoulemme, France.

| 83 | **Shift Recordings** | The background imagery is adapted from a photograph of a 747 emergency exit, with circular arrow.

| 92, 93 | **Lifestyles 2000** | The Daily Express launched the Lifestyles 2000 campaign with tube and bus shelter posters accompanied by three animated TV spots.

| 95 | **Megapixels** | *Digit* magazine covers generally feature a pretty girl. That's it. This piece is almost concept-free.

| 99 | **Fireworks** | The book features poems by the likes of Michael Palin, Spike Milligan and Christina Rosetti.

| 100 | **Advertising's biggest client** | There really are no excuses. If you advertised unsafe sex or drug use you'd kill fewer people.

| 101 | **Reckless** | Once you've bought your washing machine, you can ski in your underwear.

| 103 | **Stock Aitken Waterman** | ...who here borrow heavily from the Godfather of Soul, Mr. James Brown. Art directed by John Warwicker.

| 103-6 | **Deadline** | This magazine was produced on a tiny budget which necessitated the extensive use of images supplied free by record companies. This did, however, give us the freedom to be as cavalier with them as we wished, safe in the knowledge that an irate photographer would not be on the phone when the issue hit the shops. However, as the only proof produced before printing was of the cover, the magazine was sometimes just as much a surprise to myself and the editor. Most of these issues were produced in three days flat. Late night sustenance by Starburger and Häagen Dazs. Frank Wynne, the editor, scanned in his pack of indigestion tablets for the contents spread.

| 110 | **Demon Records** | Demon Records have a sub-label called Edsel. The cover moves onto (and off) the back cover, and the story continues on the inner pages.

| 112 | **Nanotechnology in the design office** | Lilliputian molecules tie down the old school tools.

| 113 | **Coping with future petrol shortages** | Wanna score some gas?

| 114 | **Future Transport** | Sadly, the personal jetpack always seems to be some way off.

| 117 | **MillenniumGreetings** | FontShop Australia's christmas card. The story of the new year in little icons, laid out as a fontographer sample. This is now a real Device font.

| 119 | **Goatsucker** | The Goatsucker is a South American mystery beast of recent years with a taste for sucking goat's blood. Is it a devil, an extraterrestrial or a marketing opportunity?

| 128 | **Knobcheese** | Swiss cheese with knobs on.

| 129 | **Menswear** | The ideal font for typesetting profanities.

| 129 | **Revolver** | A digitised version of the font developed in 1990 for *Revolver* magazine. It's slogan, "Where Dan Dare meets Jimi Hendrix", was the conceptual starting point. The original was drawn on board and statted to size for pasteup.

| 129 | **Identification** | Each character comes in semaphore, morse, frequency and character versions, which can be intermixed or overlaid.

| 132-3 | **Space Lounge / Riviera Fling** | Polyester loungecore attire.

| 135 | **She's gorgeous... but she stinks!** | Great copywriting by Ammirati Puris Lintas.

| 136-8 | **Tangent Comics** | The Tangent series took familiar names from the DC Universe and reinvented them from scratch: "the only thing you know is the name". The second year's set did the same with DC's heavy hitters.

| 144 | **Pit Crew 2000** | The official shirt of the Deathrace 2000 pit crew?

| 145 | **Edinburgh Independent Television Festival** | The logo features a variety of poses for use on merchandise.

| 145 | **The Reaper** | Masthead for a proposed obituary magazine.

| 145 | **The Invisibles** | The lack of logo – the lettering is the negative space.

| 148 | **Titan Books** | SF and comic book publisher's logo. Titan is a moon of Saturn, seen here edge on.

| 148 | **Manowar** | An early LP sleeve logo for a lycra and broadsword band.

| 148 | **Lord Jim** | *The Doors* logo remixed for a serial in *Crisis* magazine.

| 149 | **Paper and Ink** | The shape of the sheet of paper is only apparent in this logo because of the coloured ink splots.

| 155 | **Hed Kandi** | Mark Doyle of Jazz FM used to run a legendary club night in the early 1980's. He came to my attention because his flyer lifted imagery from my Roadblock sleeve. However, free entry was arranged and fifteen years later on this one was properly commissioned and paid for. And the music was fantastic.

| 156 | **The Observer** | Several designers were asked to submit ideas for an update of the Observer masthead. Sadly, none of these were chosen.

| 156 | **Mathengine** | "Be God. Play Dice." was my slogan for this software engine that allows modelling of real-world physical effects like gravity, softness and bounce for computer game developers. When confronted with Heisenberg's Uncertainty Principle, Einstein famously said "God does not play dice with the Universe". But now you can.

| 157 | **Tales from Beyond Science** | Original pre-digital PMT with chemical discolouration and light meter arm exposed at the top.

| 160 | **Spiderman** | I presented over 80 logo concepts for this film; this is a record for me. Here is a small selection. None were chosen.

| 161 | **XS** | This unused design was adapted to become the Baby Doc logo.

| 161 | **Device rubdown** | My digital font foundry's homage to the Letraset age.

| 161 | **My Little Pony** | Hasbro wanted to reposition the brand with a kitsch adult / teen marketing crossover in the same vein as Hello Kitty. These were some of the characters for the proposal, which also included a written document. Hair, ponies, grooming, princes and princesses, wishing wells and rainbows – My Little Pony is a work of conceptual genius. It's the Anti-Action Man.

| 162 | **Astralasia** | Trance meets the crop circle. Back to the Planet!

| 165 | **2000AD** | Steve Cook, art director of *2000AD*, mentioned that he was redesigning the classic logo. That night I saw this in a dream, on a bright yellow Brendan McCarthy cover. It was used on Parallel Earth 428X, where the circulation of the weekly comic is in the high millions. Here it remains an unpublished curiosity.

| 165 | **Mambo** | Not the Australian surfing gear manufacturer unfortunately, but a comic series by Dave Hine from 2000AD.

| 167 | **Concord** | College flashback.

| 170 | **Millennium Bug** | This is the original Millennium Bug design. It was altered and adapted by the commissioning agency. Subsequently it was passed on to a second agency who changed it yet again - in some repects back closer to this original version. They won awards.

| 170 | **Camden Mix** | Logo proposal for a free North London music festival.

| 174-5 | **Metropolitan Music** | The sleeve photographs were shot around the Hayward Gallery, which was chosen for it's brutal modern austerity. This mirrored the hard electronic nature of the music. The double-M logo again suggests an architectural perspective, maybe the corner of a building.

| 176 | **Mixed Ability** | An invitation that gives you a chance to rate the exhibitors.

| 177 | **Danny Rampling** | Spangly CDs and spongy cover for the Shoom guru.

| 178 | **Night and Day** | A special watch with only the hours of the inveterate clubber marked; comes with a compass so you can find your way home.

|180 | **Lucy Skye** | As well as reams of denim and suede, a denim jacket and jeans were also unstitched, printed with the logo repeat, and remade for Lucy.

|186 | **Outbreaks of Violets** | On the MTV Europe Awards night a copy was placed on every seat in the auditorium. The serried rows of identical brochures had the effect of looking like some weird kind of art installation. This edition is held together with two screws; these can be easily undone, and the floor of the after-show party was fully carpeted with loose pages by the end of the night. Order to chaos in six hours.
Winner of a Broadcast Design Awards Gold, 1996, and the Creative Use of Print Award, 1996. The per-unit budget of the limited edition (500 copies) was an unusual £50. This was a great opportunity to work with some personal favourite comic artists, and possibly the rarest of all Alan Moore collectables.

|194 | **Dare** | *Dare* recast Frank Hampson's 50's British sf icon Dan Dare as an innocent pawn in a political power game. "A work of simple atmospheric beauty", said the New Musical Express. "An iconoclastic revamp of the '50s comic hero" said Time Out. The roughs here are done as all roughs once were – with a mixture of cut paper, paint, Magic Marker and spray mount.

|196 | **The Invisibles** | It has become a common marketing strategy to issue a single comic in a variety of different, sometimes enhanced covers. *The Invisibles* issue 5 was released with four "dehanced" covers, A-D, in two colours on recycled stock.

|198-9 | **On the Line** | A selection of Compuserve advertorial strips from *The Guardian's* On Line computer section.

|218-9 | **Guy Ornadel** | *Licensed to Thrill* continues the James Bond action adventure theme with Guy Ornadel. So someone *does* have a jetpack...

|224 | **The Nuttiest Thing** | Art directed by Marcus Benton, this poster series had four related TV commercials in which the type was animated.

|235 | **Ellipses** | Dave Langford's story in *More Tales from The Forbidden Planet* purports to feature transcripts of channelled messages relayed from the afterlife; missing passages are indicated by ellipses (...). This is also a metaphor for the elliptical shape of a halo. The image was constructed by manipulating pages of the actual manuscript – the dead looking out at us through the medium of the written word.

|238-9 | **Transient 8** | The photographic raw material was taken along the Westway, London.

|240 | **Lost episodes** | Spock's Arse?

|243 | **Kid Eternity** | The glasses are spot-varnished; their highlights (the many-pointed Chaos symbol) are in silver ink.

|244 | **Spot the Stunt** | Copywriting that does exactly what it says on the tin courtesy of agency Triangle.

|244 | **Planet X** | Resistant to 50,000 atmospheres – and now available here on Planet Earth!

|246 | **Original audio** | With the invention of the digital CD and the Compact Disc logo, we needed one for our trusty old analogue black vinyl.

|247 | **XTC** | *Drums and Wireless* tips the hat to XTC's album *Drums and Wires*.

|251 | **Love and Rockets** | One of my personal favourite strips, this redesign for the UK market was an opportunity to better present the Hernandez' ground-breaking barrio-life soap opera. The original US collections were steeped in comic design clichés, preventing them from gaining the mass-market crossover and the more sophisticated audience they deserved. These British edition covers were actually considered somewhat daring, but soon the US publisher was following suit. This problem – inappropriate genre design for avant-garde comics – still plagues the industry. If they are to be perceived as part of a relevant pop or literature culture, they have got to routinely forge new aesthetic ground in the same way music design does. This innovation must go deeper than the cover layout and address what is perceived by the general reader as the "comicy" look – old-fashioned garish lettering and colouring being the prime offenders. Suggestions would be a move to caps and lower case type set in non-Lichtenstein styles unique to each artist; avoiding whiz-bang effects, more sophisticated splash page lettering that is conceptually linked to the cover layout typographically; and balloon placing that is a harmonious part of the overall page composition, as in many European comics. The widespread departmentalisation of production tasks (artist, letterer, colourist) unfortunately tends to homogenise a company's output and swamp an artist's individual signature. Having said that, "playing with the old toys" design, as epitomised by *Flex Mentallo*, is an enjoyable excercise.

|252-5 | **Swatches** | Three were finally produced from the range of proposed designs shown here.

|256 | **Mashed Mellow Grooves** | The photography was shot in the Caribbean from a light aircraft.

|264 | **Superman** | Action figure sketches. Concept design for film, like the design of title sequences, has always fascinated me. Two things I would like to explore further.

|265 | **The Inheritors** | *The Inheritors* attempted to explain the funny-animal premise rationally – by assuming humans have done away with themselves in some unspecified way, leaving evolved furry creatures to wander and ponder the ruins.

|265 | **The Science Service** | The anniversary of the Festival of Britain as marketing opportunity. The theme of loss of idealism is taken up again in the later *Dare*. Is this a precognition of Millennium Dome syndrome?

|265 | **Raymond Chandler: Goldfish** | This graphic novel was completed in 1992 and unfortunately is still unpublished. 44 pages of noir shadows and loose brushwork.

|265 | **Really and Truly** | Kitsch and throwaway where *Dare* was grim and cynical, our heroes Really Amazing, Truly Something, Scuba Trooper and Johnny Zhivago try to deliver designer drugs to the East Coast Burnout before Captain Nice and the House of Fun catch up with them.

|265 | **Robohunter** | 2000AD's veteran character as scripted by ex-*Crisis* and *Revolver* editor Peter Hogan.

|265 | **The Lighted Cities** | Chris Reynolds' dream-like narratives are shown to great effect in the collection *Mauretania*, from Penguin Books.

|265 | **Visions of the Future** | Acetate overlays with letratone tints and red photo-opaque Rubylith were standard ways of hand-separating colour pre-computer.

|265 | **Spiffy Designs** | Promotional card collection, with gum. A set of 50. Very rare, only 350 sets were ever issued.

|266 | **Zit** | College-era self publishing, sold through Paul Gravett's seminal Fast Fiction small-press stand at the monthly Westminster Comic Marts. The scene drew together the artists and writers that would form the pool for *Escape*

magazine. This period is detailed in Eddie Campbell's excellent *How to be an Artist*, which features panels from my early work that I had completely forgotten.

|266 | **Norm** | Escape magazine featured much of my early strip work, notably *Dark Design* and *Selectivision*, which was printed in 3D; the issue came with free red and green glasses.

|270 | **Xpresso** | *Xpresso's* remit was to reprint the "cream of European strip art". A brave experiment from Fleetway.

|270 | **Revolver** | Dan Dare was serialised in *Revolver* magazine before being collected as a graphic novel. The seven issues also featured Brendan McCarthy and Peter Milligan's *Rogan Josh*.

|270 | **Heart Throbs** | On the back of the *Xpresso* experiment, Fleetway began translating European albums. These were redesigned for the British market.

|270 | **Hewligan's Haircut** | Hewligan has a hole in his haircut that acts as an inter-dimensional portal. The cover is a die-cut, revealing the logo on page 1.

|270 | **Soda** | Proposed magazine from Fleetway that would reprint European strips for the children's market. Unpublished.

|271 | **Sam Bronx and the Robots** | Acme followed up *The Science Service* with this reprint of Serge Clerc's album, actually the first in the Atomium 58 series in the European numbering.

|272-3 | **Crisis** | Corporate logos and camouflage convey Pat Mills' theme of Third World exploitation by multinationals. *Crisis* ultimately broadened its range of material and went from a bi-weekly to a monthly.

|273 | **Third World War** | Collects Pat Mills' and Carlos Ezquerra's strip originally serialised in *Crisis* for the American market.

|274 | **Safety On Board** | Do you know where the exits are located? The voices of Leslie Phillips, Ewan McGregor and Suzanna York will tell you.

R&D

Books, articles and exhibitions